Published and Distributed by

Chopsticks Publications Ltd.
P.O. Box 73515, Kowloon Central Post Office, Hong Kong.
116D Waterloo Road, Ground Floor, Kowloon, Hong Kong.
Tel: 3-7115989, 3-7115911.

© *Cecilia J. AU-YEUNG*

1st print January 1986

ISBN 962-7018-41-4
Photography by Wilson Au-yeung
     Au-yeung Chiu Mei
Edited by Caroline Au-yeung
Designed by Lord Unit Design and Production
Krups kitchen equipment provided by Cheong Hing Store Ltd.

出版者及總批發
嘉饌出版有限公司
香港　九龍中央郵箱73515號
香港　九龍窩打老道116號D地下
電話：3-7115911，3-7115989

Foreword

Most people imagine that Chinese cooking is a difficult task, which is why so many people, including Chinese, never attempt to cook a Chinese dish.

Although the majority of Chinese dishes are easy to learn but difficult to perfect, there are also many other dishes which are quite simple. It is a common misconception that Chinese cooking is an unpleasant and messy process. If you take a step-by-step approach to Chinese cooking and start with basic and simple recipes before gradually moving on to more complicated dishes, you will find that Chinese cooking is an enjoyable experience. With the help of modern kitchen equipment, you can also avoid a great deal of mess and trouble. You should begin by learning to recognise the different ingredients, seasoning and cooking utensils, then learn to understand the correct stove temperatures and timing and so on. In this way, you will discover the wide variety of Chinese recipes and have fun while you are learning to cook. There are so many different styles of Chinese cooking that you could spend a lifetime learning them.

To show that there are simple and easy-to-follow recipes, I have especially written this book, 'First Steps in Chinese Cooking', in order to introduce a variety of delicious recipes that even children can learn. Children must, of course, be supervised by an adult to begin with, until they are older and totally familiar and at ease with their cooking environment. I would also advise parents to learn to cook these Chinese dishes with their children, so that you may share the fun of cooking and enhance your relationships through shared interests. It is important to give children a certain degree of independence and responsibility in the kitchen. You will be surprised at how much they can achieve by themselves. I have met children who are more interested in cooking than their parents and their success rate is quite high. So give them a chance to enjoy cooking Chinese food from an early age.

However, parents should be aware of potential dangers in the kitchen and keep an eye on the children when they are cooking. Check all the stoves, equipment and utensils to ensure that they work properly and are safe to use. This may be done by the parents themselves or, better still, by a professional. Unless the children are familiar with the use of a gas stove, I would suggest that they use an electric cooker. A flat-bottomed wok with a wooden handle may be used on an electric cooker. Alternatively, a simple frying pan is adequate. Although I mainly use a wok for deep frying, I would suggest that children use a Western deep-fryer with a lid since it is safer.

You will notice that in this cookery book, I have often used Western kitchen equipment, utensils and ingredients so that children will not feel that cooking Chinese food is so unusual. Indeed, some Western equipment helps to make life easier for the keen Chinese cook and Western ingredients, when used with imagination, can enhance the flavour of Chinese dishes and create new dishes.

I will also introduce to you all the common Chinese ingredients, seasoning and utensils. Do not be put off if you do not have everything you need. Most things can be substituted by something else. For beginners, the majority of the cooking utensils and equipment in an ordinary Western kitchen are sufficient.

For children, the most difficult technique in Chinese cooking is the making of a gravy, so I have collaborated many recipes with little or no gravy in this book. However, if you wish to add gravy to your food, all you need to do is follow these instructions:-

1. Put some oil in the wok;
2. Sauté the garlic, shallots and ginger;
3. Put in the ingredients to stir fry quickly;
4. Drop in the wine;
5. Trickle in the stock;
6. Finally quickly blend in the cornflour and water mixture and dish.

General Kitchen Rules

1. An adult must be present at all times when children are cooking. It is a good idea for the adult to light the stove and to remove the utensils from the stove if they are too heavy for the children to lift.

2. Remember to keep your hands clean and wear an apron while you are cooking.

3. Read the first few pages of this cookery book and familiarise yourself with the ingredients, seasoning and utensils before you begin cooking.

4. Read the recipe once from beginning to end before you start cooking to make sure you have everything you need.

5. Weigh the ingredients carefully, especially for the dim sum and dessert recipes.

6. When measuring teaspoons, tablespoons and cups in this cookery book, fill the spoon or cup and level off with a chopstick or the back of a knife.

7. Instead of using a Chinese cleaver, you may use a small knife for cutting up ingredients.

8. Use oven proof dishes in the oven or steamer and put them on heat-resistant surfaces afterwards.

9. The water must be boiling before you put the dish in the steamer for steaming. The second tier of the steamer should be used for steaming to prevent the water from boiling over and spilling into the dish.

10. Preheat the oven to the right temperature about 15 minutes before use.

11. Always use an oven cloth or glove to remove hot things from the oven or stove. A wok handle can get very hot during cooking.

12. Do not just rely on your memory to check the time, always use a timer.

13. Wash those utensils which only need rinsing while you are waiting for the dish to cook. Keep greasy pots and plates on one side to be cleaned after the meal.

14. Remember to clean everything after you have finished and return all used items to their proper places in the kitchen.

入廚須知

1. 當小朋友們開始在廚房內工作時，必須由一名成年人陪同協助一切。尤其是打火或移動笨重的器皿及沸熱的東西，更應由成年人幫助進行。
2. 煮菜時經常要穿上圍裙及記着常常洗手。
3. 先將這本書頭數頁熟讀，以便認識材料，調味和器皿方開始煮食。
4. 未開始前，先將菜譜小心讀一次。然後把材料，調味及用具準備妥當。
5. 使用磅秤時必須準確，切勿將用料加多或減少，尤其是點心及餅食絕對不能將材料增減以致影響製成品。
6. 用量匙要小心，把材料或調味盛滿後必須用刀刮平。
7. 如你不習慣用中國菜刀，可以改用小刀切材料。
8. 用來蒸或焗的盆碟必須檢查是耐燒而無裂痕的。而從爐中取出時要安放在木架或厚墊上，絕不能隨便放在普通的桌子或玻璃面。
9. 蒸餸必須預先將鑊內的水煮沸才把蒸籠架在上面大火蒸至所需的時間。最好將碟放在第二格蒸籠內以免入水。
10. 如需用焗爐，必先在入爐前十五分鐘預先妥準確度數。
11. 經常將焗爐手套或厚墊布放在廚房內當眼的地方以便隨時取用。因為焗爐內的器皿或鑊柄都是滾燙的物件，絕對不能用肉手去碰。
12. 切勿過信自己的記憶，不要單憑記性來計時。廚房內必須設有計時器以便提醒你時間到了以免食物煮焦。
13. 當烹飪進行而你需要等候時，先將不肥膩的用具以水沖淨放回原處。肥膩的器皿則留至飯後與其他碗碟一起清洗。
14. 烹飪完畢的善後工作必須由自己完成。並將曾用過的東西洗淨放回原處，不要養成依賴別人善後的壞習慣。

Content 目錄：

Baked Chicken Livers
豉 油 焗 鷄 肝

Ingredients:

12 oz (336 g) chicken livers
½ oz (14 g) ginger
2 shallots
2 garlic cloves
3 tbsp honey
1 tsp sesame oil

Marinade -
2 tbsp dark soy
2 tbsp light soy
1 tbsp red food colouring
   (optional)
2 tbsp sugar
1 tbsp rose wine or cooking sherry

Method:

* Wash and towel dry the chicken livers.
* Chop the ginger, shallots and garlic coarsely, then blend into a purée with a food processor. Scrape the purée on to a saucer.
* Mix the marinade with the purée and stir until the sugar dissolves. Coat the livers thoroughly with the mixed marinade. Leave aside to soak for an hour.
* Preheat the oven to 400°F (Gas Mark 6).
* Line an oblong baking tray with tin foil and top it with a greased rack.
* Arrange the livers on the rack and place it in the middle shelf of the oven to bake for 10 minutes. Remove and coat with the honey. Turn the livers and bake it in the oven for a further 10 minutes. Turn off the heat and remove the livers on to a chopping board. Brush with sesame oil then slice into thick pieces and arrange on a platter. Serve hot or cold.

材料：
鷄肝12安（336克）
羗½安（14克）
葱頭 2 粒
蒜頭 2 粒
蜜糖 3 湯匙
蔴油 1 茶匙塗面

醃料 —
老抽 2 湯匙
生抽 2 湯匙
紅粉水 1 湯匙
糖 2 湯匙
酒 1 湯匙

製法：

＊　鷄肝洗淨以毛巾吸乾水份。
＊　羗、葱、蒜頭全部切開，放入攪拌器中打爛成泥，以膠刮刮出放在一個深碟上。
＊　醃料加在碟中與羗、葱、蒜泥一同攪拌至糖溶。即將鷄肝放入反覆沾滿醃料。置一旁醃 1 小時。
＊　焗爐預開至400度（煤氣6度）
＊　長方焗盆一個內鋪錫紙。上面架一塗油鐵絲網或不銹鋼架，將鷄肝排放在鐵網上。放入焗爐中格焗10分鐘。取出淋以蜜糖。反轉重放爐內再焗10分鐘。熄去爐火將鷄肝取出塗上蔴油，切厚件上碟。

Baked Chicken Wings
鹽 水 焗 鷄 翼

Ingredients:

1 lb (½ kg) chicken wings
5 cups water
1 oz (28 g) ginger
3 shallots
3 star anises
1 tbsp sesame oil for coating

Seasoning-
2 tbsp wine
3 tbsp salt
1 cube chicken essence
2 tbsp sugar

Method:

* Blanch and wash the chicken wings thoroughly. Refresh and drain. Cut 2 slits on the thick meaty part near the joints.
* Bring the water to boil in a 3 quart saucepan. Scrape and slice the ginger. Peel and crush the shallots and star anises. Add all these to the water. Reduce the heat and continue to boil for 20 minutes till the flavour comes out.
* Pour all the seasoning into the water. Slide in the chicken wings. When the water reboils, turn off the heat. Leave the chicken wings to stand in the salted water for 20 minutes. Remove and drain off the excess water. Brush with the sesame oil.
* Sit a greased rack on a baking tray and arrange the chicken wings on the rack. Place the whole tray in a preheated oven of 450°F (Gas Mark 8) to bake for 6 minutes. Remove the tray from the oven and turn the wings over to bake the other side for 5 minutes or till golden brown.

材料：
鷄翼 1 磅（ ½ 公斤 ）
水 5 杯
羗 1 安（ 28克 ）
葱頭 3 粒
八角 3 粒
蔴油 1 湯匙塗面

調味—
酒 2 湯匙
鹽 3 湯匙
鷄精 1 粒
糖 2 湯匙

製法：

＊ 鷄翼以沸水洗淨，擦去油污，隔乾水份。每隻在厚肉處輕鎅兩刀。

＊ 深鍋 1 隻將水傾入以中火煮沸。羗刮皮切片。葱頭去衣拍扁與八角一同加在沸水中，轉用文火煮20分鐘至出味。

＊ 調味料全部傾入沸水中煮溶，即將鷄翼放入，待水再滾時，熄去爐火。留下鷄翼在鹽水中浸20分鐘。取出隔清鹽水，塗以蔴油。

＊ 烤盆一隻上放塗油鐵線架，將鷄翼排在架上。放入已預熱之猛火焗爐內450度（煤氣8度）焗約 6 分鐘。取出反轉再焗 5 分鐘即成。

Chicken and Vegetable Kebabs

串 燒 鷄

Ingredients:

8 oz (224 g) chicken fillet
2 slices ginger
2 garlic cloves

2 shallots
4 oz (112 g) cucumber
4 oz (112 g) tomatoes
3 tbsp oil for brushing

Marinade-
1 tsp ginger juice
1 tsp wine
1 tsp curry powder
1 tbsp tomato ketchup
1 tbsp Worchestershire sauce
1 tbsp peanut butter
¼ tsp salt
1 tsp sugar
1 tsp light soy
½ tsp black pepper
¼ cup water
1 tsp cornflour
½ tbsp sesame oil, to be added last

Special Utensils:

24 skewers

Method:

* Wash, dry and dice the chicken into ½"(1.25 cm) cubes.
* Mince the ginger, garlic and shallots. Put into a mixing bowl and stir well with the above marinade (except the sesame oil). Immerse the chicken to stand for 30 minutes then blend in the sesame oil to marinate for a further 30 minutes.
* Wash, deseed and dice the cucumber. Wash and dice the tomatoes into similar size to the cucumber.
* Skewer a piece each of chicken, cucumber and tomato alternately. Put on a greased rack in a baking tray and bake for 5 minutes in a preheated 400°F (Gas Mark 6) oven. Remove and brush with the oil. Return into the oven to bake for another 5 minutes until golden brown. Serve hot.

N.B. The tomatoes in this recipe can be substituted by carrots, the latter should be blanched and diced before use.

材料：

鷄肉 8 安（224克）
羌 2 片
蒜頭 2 粒
葱頭 2 粒
青瓜 4 安（112克）
番茄或甘笋 4 安（112克）
油 3 湯匙掃面

醃料一
羌汁 1 茶匙　　　糖 1 茶匙
酒 1 茶匙　　　　生抽 1 茶匙
咖喱粉 1 茶匙　　黑胡椒½茶匙
茄汁 1 湯匙　　　水¼杯
喼汁 1 湯匙　　　生粉 1 茶匙
花生醬 1 湯匙　　蔴油½湯匙（後下）
鹽¼茶匙

竹籤或鋼針 2 打

製法：

* 鷄肉洗淨抹乾切成約½吋（1.25 公分）丁方粒。
* 羌、蒜頭、葱頭去衣剁茸放在大碗中，與上述醃料（除蔴油）一同和勻。加入鷄粒撈勻醃約30分鐘，將蔴油拌入再醃30分鐘。
* 青瓜洗淨去籽切丁方粒。番茄亦洗淨切同樣大小粒候用。
* 竹籤或鋼針塗油穿上一粒鷄肉，一粒青瓜；第二粒鷄肉，1粒番茄；再穿最後 1 粒鷄肉，放在已塗油之架上盛在焗盤中，置已預熱 400 度（煤氣 6 度）焗爐內焗 5 分鐘；取出塗油放回爐中再焗 5 分鐘至金黃色即成。共得串燒鷄約 2 打。
註：如用甘笋可先飛水而後切粒。

Deep Fried Chicken Thighs

五香炸鶏腿

12

Ingredients:

4 chicken thighs, about 6 oz (168 g) each
1 tbsp five spice powder
1 tbsp minced garlic
1 tbsp minced shallots
1 tbsp minced ginger
a few cups oil for deep frying

Marinade-
1 tbsp wine
1 tbsp ginger juice
2 tbsp fermented red beancurd
3 tbsp dark soy
5 tbsp sugar
½ tsp chicken essence
1 tsp cornflour
3 tbsp water

Method:

* Wash and dry the chicken thighs. Slash 2 to 3 slits on each side.
* Place all the remaining ingredients except the oil in a mixing bowl. Add the seasoning and stir until the sugar dissolves. Marinate the chicken for 1 hour, turning them occasionally.
* Slowly bring the oil to boil. Put in the chicken thighs to deep fry over low heat until both sides are golden and thoroughly cooked. Drain on the kitchen paper and serve hot.

材料：

雞腿 4 隻每隻約 6 安（168克）
五香粉 1 湯匙
蒜茸 1 湯匙
葱頭茸 1 湯匙
羌茸 1 湯匙
炸油數杯

醃料—
酒 1 湯匙
羌汁 1 湯匙
南乳 2 湯匙
老抽 3 湯匙
糖 5 湯匙
雞粉 ½ 茶匙
生粉 1 茶匙
水 3 湯匙

製法：

* 雞腿洗淨抹乾，用刀在雞腿兩面各剠 2 至 3 條刀紋。
* 五香粉、蒜、葱、羌茸與醃料和勻。將糖拌溶後試妥味把雞腿放入醃 1 小時。
* 慢火將油燒沸後將雞腿放入文火炸至深黃色及熟透。撈起隔去油，即可上碟。

Shredded Chicken with Oyster Sauce

蠔 油 手 撕 鷄

Ingredients:

2 chicken thighs,
  about 8 oz (224 g) each
½ oz (14 g) agar agar
1 oz (28 g) toasted peanuts
2 spring onions

Chicken Marinade-
2 tbsp ginger juice
2 tbsp wine
⅓ tsp salt
1 tsp sugar

Seasoning-
¼ cup stock
3 tbsp oyster sauce
1 tsp sugar
¼ tsp pepper
1 tsp sesame oil

Method:

* Rinse the chicken thighs with boiling water and pat dry with a clean towel. Slash 3 slits lengthwise on each side and place on to a platter.

* Mix the marinade thoroughly in a small bowl. Pour half of the marinade on to one side of the chicken thighs and turn over the other side to coat with the remaining marinade. Leave aside to soak for an hour. Turn the thighs over every 20 minutes. Place in a steamer to cook for 12 minutes. Remove and leave aside to cool. Tear the flesh into thick strips of similar size to the agar agar.

* Wash the agar agar in warm water and towel dry. Cut into 2″ (5 cm) lengths and arrange on a platter. Top with the chicken shreds.

* Crush the peanuts. Wash and dice the spring onions.

* Clean a small saucepan and pour in the mixed seasoning to bring to boil. Season to taste and scoop on to the chicken. Sprinkle with the crushed peanuts and spring onions and serve cold.

材料：

鷄腿 2 隻共約 1 磅（ ½ 公斤 ）
大菜絲 ½ 安（ 14克 ）
脆花生 1 安（ 28克 ）
葱 2 棵

醃鷄料一
羌汁 2 湯匙
酒 2 湯匙
鹽 ⅓ 茶匙
糖 1 茶匙

調味一
上湯 ¼ 杯
蠔油 3 湯匙
糖 1 茶匙
古月粉 ¼ 茶匙
蔴油 1 茶匙

製法：

* 鷄腿以沸水洗淨。每邊斜切三刀，放在碟上。

* 醃鷄料放在小碗內拌匀，先淋一半在鷄腿之一邊。反轉鷄腿，將其餘一半醃料平均倒下放置一旁醃 1 小時。中途將鷄腿轉身 2 次使入味。置蒸籠內蒸12分鐘。取出攤凍撕成鷄條，粗幼與大菜相等。

* 大菜絲用溫水洗淨。剪爲 2 吋小段。排放在平碟上。將鷄條鋪在上面。

* 脆花生樁碎，葱洗淨切粒。

* 小鍋一個洗淨，將調味料和匀傾入文火煮沸。試妥味後淋在鷄肉上。再灑花生碎及葱粒鋪面。即可上桌。

Shredded Chicken with Red Cabbage

紅 椰 菜 鷄 絲

Ingredients:

5 oz (140 g) chicken fillet
10 oz (280 g) red cabbage
2 slices ginger

1 garlic clove
2 spring onions
3 tbsp oil

Chicken Marinade-
1 tsp ginger juice
1 tsp wine
$1/8$ tsp salt
$1/4$ tsp sugar
1 tsp cornflour
1 tbsp water
1 tsp sesame oil, to be added last

Seasoning-
$1/4$ tsp salt
2 tbsp stock
1 tsp light soy
$1/2$ tsp sugar

Method:

* Shred the chicken fillet into $1\frac{1}{2}''$ x $\frac{1}{4}''$(4 cm x 1 cm) strips and put into the above marinade (except the sesame oil) to stand for 30 minutes. Blend in the sesame oil and leave aside for a further 30 minutes.
* Wash and slice the red cabbage. Shred the ginger. Slice the garlic. Section the spring onions. Put all these ingredients on a platter for later use.
* Heat the pan or wok to bring half the oil to boil. Sauté the ginger and stir in the chicken to fry until the chicken meat turns white. Remove and drain.
* Heat another wok and bring the remaining oil to boil. Slide in the garlic to sauté till fragrant. Pour in the red cabbage and salt to stir fry for a while then add the shredded chicken to toss well. Sprinkle in the stock gradually to mix thoroughly. Season to taste. Scatter the spring onions on top and dish.

材料：

雞胸肉 5 安（140克）
紅椰菜10安（280克）
羌 2 片
蒜頭 1 粒
葱 2 棵
油 3 湯匙

醃雞料 —
羌汁 1 茶匙
酒 1 茶匙
鹽 $\frac{1}{8}$ 茶匙
糖 $\frac{1}{4}$ 茶匙
生粉 1 茶匙
水 1 湯匙
蔴油 1 茶匙（後下）

調味 —
鹽 $\frac{1}{4}$ 茶匙
上湯 2 湯匙
生抽 1 茶匙
糖 $\frac{1}{2}$ 茶匙

製法：

* 雞胸肉切$1\frac{1}{2}$吋（4公分）×$\frac{1}{4}$吋（1公分）粗條。放在和勻之醃料中拌妥置一旁$\frac{1}{2}$小時。加入蔴油攪勻再醃$\frac{1}{2}$小時。
* 紅椰菜洗淨切粗條。羌切絲，蒜頭切片，葱切度。全部配料放在碟上候用。
* 煎鍋或鑊洗淨燒熱，將一半油傾入爆香羌絲，隨即把雞絲放入炒勻至肉變白色，即可盛起。
* 另鑊燒熱將其餘一半油倒下煮沸，滑下蒜片爆香即將椰菜傾入灑鹽炒片刻。加入雞絲拌炒數下。將上湯邊炒邊灑入。再將其餘調味料放入兜勻。試妥味，灑葱度攪勻上碟。

Steamed Chicken with Sausages

臘 腸 蒸 鷄

Ingredients:

10 oz (280 g) chicken thigh or breast
2 oz (56 g) fresh mushrooms
2 Chinese sausages or pork sausages

1 tbsp shredded ginger
1 tbsp shredded spring onions

Chicken Marinade-
1 tsp ginger juice
1 tsp wine

Seasoning-
¼ tsp salt
1½ tsp sugar
1 tbsp oyster sauce
1 tbsp soy sauce
a pinch of pepper
1 tsp cornflour
1 tbsp water
1 tsp sesame oil

Method:

* Clean, debone and cut the chicken into bite-sized pieces. Mix in the above marinade and leave aside for 20 minutes. Blend in all the seasoning to marinate for another 20 minutes.
* Wash, trim and slice the mushrooms into thick pieces. Wash and slice the sausages.
* Place the marinated chicken, mushrooms and sausages on a platter. Add an extra tsp of water and 1 tbsp of oil to mix well. Arrange in a steamer to cook for 12 minutes over moderate heat. Remove and sprinkle the shredded ginger and spring onions on top. Serve hot.

材料：

鷄脾或胸肉10安（280克）
白菌 2 安（56克）
腊腸或香腸 2 條
羗絲 1 湯匙
葱絲 1 湯匙

醃鷄料—
羗汁 1 茶匙
酒 1 茶匙

調味—
鹽 ¼ 茶匙
糖 1½ 茶匙
蠔油 1 湯匙
生抽 1 湯匙
古月粉少許
生粉 1 茶匙
水 1 湯匙
蔴油 1 茶匙

製法：

* 鷄胸肉洗淨去骨切件。以上述醃料和勻醃20分鐘後，加入全部調味料撈勻再醃20分鐘。
* 白菌洗淨修妥切厚片。腊腸洗淨切片。
* 將鷄肉，白菌片，腊腸片一同放在深碟中。拌入額外清水 1 茶匙及油 1 湯匙撈勻。置蒸籠內以中火蒸12分鐘。取出灑下羗絲及葱絲。上桌熟食。

Braised Ribs in Soy Sauce
簡 易 炆 排 骨

Ingredients:

1 lb (½ kg) spare ribs
4 ginger slices
4 shallots
3 cups water
1 tbsp wine
2 tbsp red vinegar
3 tbsp sugar
4 tbsp dark soy
5 tbsp water
2 tbsp diced spring onions
1 tsp sesame oil

Method:

* Wash and chop the spare ribs into 3″ (7½ cm) lengths.
* Mash the ginger. Peel and mash the shallots.
* Bring the water to boil and put in half of the ginger and shallots and all the spare ribs to blanch for 1 minute. Rinse it under a running tap and drain.
* Pour the wine, vinegar, sugar, dark soy, water and the remaining ginger and shallots into a casserole or a saucepan to bring to boil over moderate heat. Pour in the blanched spare ribs and simmer over low heat for 30 to 40 minutes until tender. Sprinkle with the spring onions and sesame oil and serve in the casseroles.

材料：

肉排 1 磅（½公斤）
羗 4 片
葱頭 4 粒
水 3 杯
酒 1 湯匙
浙醋 2 湯匙
沙糖 3 湯匙
老抽 4 湯匙
水 5 湯匙
葱花 2 湯匙灑面
蔴油 1 茶匙

製法：

* 肉排洗淨將每支骨劃開斬成 3 吋（7½公分）段。
* 羗拍扁，葱頭去衣略拍。
* 水煮沸加一半羗片葱頭及全部排骨飛水，洗淨隔去水份。
* 瓦鍋或不銹鋼鍋一個，將酒、醋、糖、豉油及水與其餘羗葱一同放入中火煮沸。隨將已出水之排骨放入文火炆30至40分鐘至酥軟。灑葱花蔴油原鍋上桌。

Diced Ham with Cashew Nuts

腰 果 腿 丁

Ingredients:

5 oz (140 g) ham
6 cooked mushrooms
1 apple
2 cups water + 1 tsp salt

2 oz (56 g) broccoli
2 oz (56 g) carrots
3 oz (84 g) cashew nuts
2 tbsp oil
1 slice ginger
1 shallot

Seasoning-
¼ tsp salt
½ tsp wine
¼ cup water
2 tsp light soy
1 tsp sugar
a pinch of pepper

Gravy-
½ tsp cornflour
1 tbsp water
¼ tsp dark soy
½ tsp sesame oil

Method:

* Dice the ham and mushrooms.
* Peel, core, dice and soak the apple in the water with salt to prevent it from discolouring. Drain and keep the salted water for later use.
* Wash and dice the broccoli. Peel and dice the carrots. Boil both the ingredients in the above salted water for half a minute. Remove and rinse with cold water. Keep the salted water.
* Reboil the above salted water and cook the cashew nuts for 3 minutes and drain. Place into a preheated oven of 250°F (Gas Mark ½) and bake for 30 minutes. Alternatively, deep fry in cool oil over low heat until light brown.
* Heat the wok with the above oil. Saute the ginger and shallot until fragrant and discard. Pour in all the diced ingredients and add the salt to stir rapidly. Sprinkle wine, add the water and seasoning. Thicken the sauce with the gravy mix. Lastly, stir in the cashew nuts to mix well. Dish and serve.

材料：

火腿5安（140克）
熟冬菇6隻
萍果1個
水2杯＋鹽1茶匙
芥蘭莖2安（56克）
甘笋2安（56克）
腰果3安（84克）
油2湯匙
羌1片
葱頭1粒

調味—
鹽¼茶匙
酒½茶匙
水¼杯
生抽2茶匙
糖1茶匙
古月粉少許

饋料—
生粉½茶匙
水1湯匙
老抽¼茶匙
蔴油½茶匙

製法：

* 火腿及熟冬菇切粒。
* 萍果去皮去心切粒以鹽水2杯浸着以防變色。30分鐘後把鹽水傾出候用。
* 芥蘭莖洗淨切粒。甘笋去皮切粒將芥蘭與甘笋粒同放上述2杯鹽水中煮½分鐘。撈起以冷水洗淨。
* 腰果亦放沸鹽水中煮3分鐘。撈起隔去水份吹乾，放在已預熱之250度（煤氣½度）焗爐內焗30分鐘；或以慢火凍油炸至金黃色。
* 鑊燒紅加油煮沸，放入羌、葱頭略爆後棄去。倒入全部粒料加鹽迅速兜勻。贊酒加水及調味料煮沸，以生粉水埋饋，加腰果撈勻上碟。

Pork and Papaya Soup

木 瓜 猪 肉 湯

Ingredients:

10 oz (280 g) lean pork
4 cups boiling water
2 slices ginger
3 to 4 dried figs
2 oz (56 g) dried mussels
a pinch of pepper
1 lb (½ kg) papayas
4 to 5 cups water

Seasoning-
1½ tsp salt

Method:

* Wash and trim the excess fat from the pork. Rinse with 3 cups of boiling water. Refresh and drain.
* Mash the ginger. Clean and halve the figs. Wash and soak the mussels in the remaining cup of boiling water. Drain and sprinkle with the pepper.
* Peel, wash and cut the papayas into large chunks.
* Fill a casserole with the water and add the pork, mussels, figs and ginger. Bring to the boil over moderate heat, then lower the heat to simmer for 30 minutes. Remove the lid and pour in the papayas to boil for another 30 minutes. Season to taste with the salt and serve hot.

材料：

瘦肉10安（280克）
羌 2 片
無花果 3 至 4 粒
淡菜乾 2 安（56克）
古月粉少許
木瓜 1 磅（ ½ 公斤 ）
水 4 至 5 杯

調味一
鹽1½茶匙

製法：

* 瘦肉洗淨，修去肥肉，以沸水重洗一次，冲凍水後隔乾。
* 羌拍扁。無花果洗淨切開邊。淡菜洗淨以水 1 杯浸 1 小時，再仔細過乾淨，灑少許古月粉撈勻。
* 木瓜削去皮洗淨切大件。
* 瓦保一個將水注入，加入瘦肉、淡菜、無花果及羌片以中火煮沸，轉用文火煮½小時。揭蓋放入木瓜續煮½小時，加鹽調妥味即可飲用。

Pork and Potato Patties
茨 仔 肉 餅

Ingredients:

10 oz (280 g) potatoes
10 oz (280 g) pork
5 oz (140 g) onions

2 eggs
½ cup flour
1 cup breadcrumbs
several tbsp oil for shallow
  frying

Seasoning-
1 tsp spicy salt
1½ tsp sugar
1 tsp wine
1 tbsp light soy
a pinch of pepper
½ tsp sesame oil
2 tsp cornflour

Method:

* Boil the potatoes in a sauce-pan till thoroughly cooked. Peel and mash into a purée.
* Mince the pork in a food processor. Clean and dice the onions finely.
* Place the potatoes, pork, onions and 1 egg into a big bowl. Stir in the seasoning to mix well. Shape into small patties.
* Beat the other egg for later use.
* Dust a little flour on to each patty then toss in the beaten egg and coat evenly with the breadcrumbs. Bring 2 tbsp oil to boil and slide in the patties to shallow fry till both sides are golden brown. Repeat this process till the mixture has been finished.

材料：

薯仔10安（280克）
豬肉10安（280克）
洋葱5安（140克）
蛋2隻
麵粉½杯
麵包糠1杯
油數湯匙煎餅用

調味—
香鹽1茶匙
糖1½茶匙
酒1茶匙
生抽1湯匙
古月粉少許
蔴油½茶匙
生粉2茶匙

製法：

* 薯仔焓熟去皮挾爛成茸。
* 豬肉剁爛。洋葱切幼粒。
* 將薯茸，肉茸及洋葱茸同放在大盆中。加蛋1隻及調味品攪勻做成小圓餅。
* 另一隻蛋打勻候用。
* 將每個小餅拍上麵粉，再放入蛋液中，然後滾上麵包糠。放油2湯匙煮沸，將餅滑入鑊中半煎炸至金黃色。剷起隔淨油，排放碟上。

Pork Chops in Orange Sauce

橙 汁 猪 扒

Ingredients:

12 oz (336 g) pork chops
1 slice ginger
1 shallot
1 egg
½ cup cornflour
½ wok oil for deep frying
1 tbsp cooked oil
1 slice orange for garnishing

Marinade-
2 tbsp light soy
2 tsp sugar
1 tsp ginger juice
1 tsp wine
1 tsp cornflour
a pinch of pepper
2 tbsp orange juice

Gravy Mix-
½ cup orange juice
¼ tsp salt
½ tsp sugar
½ tsp chicken powder
2 tsp custard powder

Method:

* Wash and pat the pork chops. Mince the ginger and shallot and blend in the marinade to mix well. Season to taste then immerse the pork chops to soak for 20 minutes. Turn over and marinate the other side for 20 minutes.
* Shell and beat the egg in a bowl. Dip the pork chops in the beaten egg to coat evenly then dust with the cornflour.
* Deep fry the pork chops in the boiling oil until golden brown. Remove, drain and arrange on to a platter.

* Mix the orange juice with the other gravy seasoning. Heat a small saucepan and pour in the gravy mix to simmer over low heat. Continue stirring with a wooden spoon until the gravy thickens. Stir in the cooked oil and pour over the pork chops. Garnish with the orange slice and serve.

材料：

豬扒12安（336克）
羌1片
葱頭1粒
蛋1隻
生粉½杯
炸油½鍋
熟油1湯匙
橙片點綴

醃料—
生抽2湯匙
糖2茶匙
羌汁1茶匙
酒1茶匙
生粉1茶匙
古月粉少許
橙汁2湯匙

饀汁—
橙汁½杯
鹽¼茶匙
糖½茶匙
鷄粉½茶匙
吉士粉2茶匙

製法：

* 豬扒洗淨拍鬆。羌、葱頭剁茸同放醃料中攪勻。試妥味將豬扒放入撈妥醃20分鐘；反轉再醃20分鐘。
* 蛋去殼打爛。將醃妥之豬扒放入捲滿蛋液；再放在生粉上沾滿乾粉。
* 油煮沸放入豬扒炸至金黃色，取出隔去餘油攤放碟上。
* 饀料全部放在碗中拌勻。不銹鋼保燒熱，將已和勻之饀料倒入文火煮杰；邊煮邊不停以木棍攪勻。最後加入熟油和勻淋在豬扒上，以橙片圍邊上桌。

Beef and Tomato Chowder

番 茄 肉 茸 羹

Ingredients:

4 oz (112 g) minced beef
10 oz (280 g) tomatoes
6 oz (168 g) beancurd
1 tbsp oil
1 slice ginger
4 cups water

1 tbsp chopped spring onions

Meat Marinade-
1 tsp sugar
2 tsp light soy
⅛ tsp dark soy
¼ tsp wine

a pinch of pepper
¼ cup water
1½ tsp cornflour
1 tbsp oil, to be added last

Seasoning-
1 tsp wine
1 tsp salt
1 tsp sugar
1 tsp chicken essence

Gravy Mix-
1½ tbsp cornflour
3 tbsp water
½ tsp dark soy

Method:

* Place all the beef marinade (except the oil) in a mixing bowl and stir until the sugar dissolves. Put in the minced beef to mix thoroughly. Leave to stand for 30 minutes. Blend in the oil and marinate for another 30 minutes.
* Wash and cut the tomatoes into ¾″ (1.8 cm) cubes. Cut the beancurd into similar size to the tomatoes. Blanch, refresh and drain.
* Heat a casserole with the oil to sauté the ginger till pungent and discard. Sizzle the wine and pour in the water and tomatoes. Simmer over moderate heat, uncovered, for 5 minutes. Add the beancurd and beef. When the water reboils, flavour it with the seasoning and thicken the sauce with the gravy mix if desired. Scatter the spring onions on top and serve in the casserole.

材料：

免治牛肉 4 安（112克）
番茄10安（280克）
豆腐 6 安（168克）
油 1 湯匙
羌 1 片
水 4 杯
葱粒 1 湯匙

醃肉料—
糖 1 茶匙
生抽 2 茶匙
老抽⅛茶匙
酒¼茶匙
古月粉少許
水¼杯
生粉1½茶匙
油 1 湯匙（後下）

調味—
酒 1 茶匙
鹽 1 茶匙
糖 1 茶匙
雞精 1 茶匙

饡料—
生粉1½湯匙
水 3 湯匙
老抽½茶匙

製法：

* 將醃肉料放在碗中和勻至糖溶，加入牛肉撈勻醃30分鐘。將油拌入再醃30分鐘。
* 番茄洗淨切成¾吋（1.8公分）丁方粒。豆腐亦切同樣大小丁方粒。將豆腐飛水洗淨隔乾水份。
* 瓦鍋燒熱加油爆香羌片棄去。贊酒倒入水及番茄以中火煮 5 分鐘。加入豆腐及牛肉。再煮滾時，將調味料放入；以生粉加水和勻，拌入煮成半稀杰之羹。灑下葱粒原煲上桌。

Corned Beef and Green Leek Patties

牛肉韭菜餅

Ingredients:

8 oz (224 g) corned beef
6 oz (168 g) green leeks
1 slice ginger

2 egg yolks
½ cup flour
a few tbsp oil for shallow
  frying

Seasoning-
¼ tsp salt
1 tsp light soy
2 tsp sugar
¼ tsp pepper
1 tbsp cornflour

Method:

* Put the corned beef in a mixing bowl and mash with a wooden spoon.

* Wash, dry and dice the green leeks. Mince the ginger finely. Add the leeks, ginger, beaten egg yolks and the seasoning to the corned beef to combine well. Season to taste.

* Sift the flour on to a platter. Shape the above mixture into small patties and coat evenly with the flour.

* Heat a pan with the oil and arrange the patties to shallow fry until both sides are golden brown. Drain and dish.

材料：

罐頭鹹牛肉 8 安（224克）
韮菜 6 安（168克）
羗 1 片
蛋王 2 隻
麵粉 ½ 杯
油數湯匙（煎餅用）

調味—
鹽 ¼ 茶匙
生抽 1 茶匙
糖 2 茶匙
古月粉 ¼ 茶匙
生粉 1 湯匙

製法：

* 牛肉放在大碗中以木匙搞爛。
* 韮菜洗淨抹乾水份切碎，羗剁成茸。一同傾下牛肉中再加已和勻之蛋王及調味料攪拌試妥味。
* 麵粉篩在平碟上，將碗中混合物以手做成小圓餅。放在粉上拖勻，使均勻地沾上麵粉。
* 平底鑊加油。將圓餅排入煎至兩面金黃色即可上碟。

Double Meatballs with Mixed Vegetables

雜菜扒雙丸

Ingredients:

5 oz (140 g) fish balls
5 oz (140 g) beef balls
3½ cups boiling water
1 cup mixed vegetables
1 slice ginger
1 shallot
2 tbsp oil

Seasoning-
¼ tsp salt
1½ tsp sugar
1 tsp wine
1 cup stock
1 tbsp light soy
a pinch of pepper

Gravy Mix-
2 tsp cornflour
2 tbsp water
¼ tsp dark soy
½ tsp sesame oil

Method:

* Blanch the fish balls and the beef balls in 2 cups of boiling water. Refresh and drain.
* Blanch the mixed vegetables in 1½ cups of boiling water. Remove, wash under the running tap and drain. Leave aside for later use.
* Peel and shred the ginger and shallot.
* Heat the wok to bring the oil to boil and sauté the ginger and shallot. Put in the mixed vegetables, fish and beef balls. Sprinkle the salt and sugar to stir fry for a while. Sizzle the wine, add the stock and seasoning to simmer for 1 minute. Season to taste. Mix the cornflour with the water and dark soy then stream into the sauce to thicken. Drop in the sesame oil to toss well. Dish and serve.

材料：

魚蛋 5 安（140克）
牛丸 5 安（140克）
沸水共3½杯
雜菜 1 杯
羌 1 片
葱頭 1 粒
油 2 湯匙

調味一
鹽¼茶匙
糖1½茶匙
酒 1 茶匙
上湯 1 杯
生抽 1 湯匙
古月粉少許

饡料一
生粉 2 茶匙
水 2 湯匙
老抽¼茶匙
蔴油½茶匙

製法：

* 魚蛋及牛丸放於 2 杯沸水中飛水，沖淨隔清水份。
* 雜菜亦放1½杯沸水中飛水，取出放水喉下沖凍，隔乾候用。
* 羌、葱頭去皮切絲。
* 燒紅鑊加油煮沸爆香羌葱絲。放入雜菜、魚蛋及牛丸、灑鹽、糖兜炒片刻。贊酒加入上湯及調味料煮 1 分鐘。試妥味以生粉加水及老抽拌勻流入和成饡汁，灑蔴油撈勻上碟。

Steamed Minced Beef
榨 菜 牛 肉 餅

Ingredients:

8 oz (224 g) beef fillet
2 oz (56 g) pickled mustard or pre-
    served vegetables
2 oz (56 g) water chestnuts
½ sq. in. (1.25 cm²) dried tangerine
    peel

1 slice ginger
2 spring onions
2 parsley sprigs
½ tsp sesame oil to grease the
    saucer

Seasoning-
¼ tsp salt
2 tsp sugar
1 tsp light soy
½ tsp wine
a pinch of pepper
⅓ cup water
1 tbsp cornflour
2 tbsp oil, to be added last

Method:

* Wash, pat dry and mince the beef fillet coarsely.
* Dice the pickled mustard.
* Peel and dice the water chestnuts.
* Wash and soak the dried tangerine peel in warm water for 30 minutes, then chop coarsely with the ginger.
* To save time, you can use a food processor to mince all the ingredients into a coarse paste.
* Put the seasoning into a mixing bowl and stir continuously till the sugar dissolves. Add the minced beef and stir with a pair of chopsticks until evenly mixed. Pour in the oil and stir again. Leave aside to marinate for 20 minutes. Shred the spring onions and trim the parsley.
* Grease a saucer with the sesame oil then spread the minced beef on the saucer to steam over medium heat for 6 to 8 minutes. Remove and sprinkle the shredded spring onions and parsley on top. Serve hot.

材料：

牛柳½磅（224克）
榨菜2安（56克）
馬蹄2安（56克）
陳皮½方吋
羌1片
葱2棵
芫茜2棵
蔴油½茶匙塗碟

調味一
鹽¼茶匙
糖2茶匙
生抽1茶匙
酒½茶匙
古月粉少許
水⅓杯
生粉1湯匙
油2湯匙（後下）

製法：

* 牛柳洗淨抹乾切成大片。置肉攪內攪成肉茸。
* 榨菜洗淨切幼粒。
* 馬蹄去皮沖淨切幼。
* 陳皮預先用暖水浸½小時與羌片切幼。如欲節省時間，可將榨菜、馬蹄、陳皮切片與牛肉同放肉攪中攪爛。以碟盛起。
* 調味料放深盆內攪拌至糖溶，試妥味將各茸放入以筷子順同一方向攪拌至均勻。加入油再攪片刻，放置一旁醃20分鐘。葱切絲芫茜摘妥。
* 深碟塗以蔴油將牛肉放入抹平，置蒸籠內猛火蒸6至8分鐘取出。葱絲與芫茜同灑在上面，即可上桌。

Prawn and Sausage Kebabs
串　燒　腸　仔　蝦

Ingredients:

10 cocktail sausages
10 medium size prawns
2 cups boiling water
4 oz (112 g) water chestnuts
   or pears
½ cucumber

Prawns Marinade-
1 tsp cornflour
¼ tsp salt
a pinch of pepper

Seasoning-
2 tbsp tomato ketchup
1 tbsp broadbean paste
1 tsp light soy
1 tsp lemon juice
1 tbsp sugar

Method:

* Remove the cocktail sausages from the can and dry them with a clean towel.
* Shell, devein, wash and dry the prawns. Prepare the marinade and sprinkle some on to each prawn. Leave to stand for 20 minutes then blanch for a few seconds in the boiling water till the prawns curl up. Remove and drain. Keep the boiling water to blanch the water chestnuts.
* Peel, trim, blanch and drain the water chestnuts. (The blanching method can be omitted if you use pears.) Partly peel the cucumber lengthwise in alternate strips. Deseed and cut into large cubes of similar size to the prawns.

* Thread the water chestnuts, sausages, prawns and cucumber alternately on a skewer. Arrange the kebabs on a preheated greased iron plate and grill for about 2 minutes. Pour the mixed seasoning over the kebabs and serve immediately.

材料：

罐頭鷄尾腸10條
中蝦10隻
馬蹄或啤梨 4 安（112克）
青瓜½條

醃蝦料 —
生粉 1 茶匙
鹽¼茶匙
古月粉少許

汁料 —
茄汁 2 湯匙
豆瓣醬 1 湯匙
生抽 1 茶匙
檸汁 1 茶匙
糖 1 湯匙

製法：

* 鷄尾腸從罐中取出隔去水份，以毛巾吸乾。
* 蝦去殼挑腸洗淨抹乾。將醃料和匀灑在蝦上拖匀，醃20分鐘後置沸水中泡片刻至剛捲起時即可撈出。
* 馬蹄去皮削圓飛水過冷河（如用啤梨則毋須飛水）。青瓜間疏去皮挖去籽切丁方粒。
* 以鋼針將馬蹄、鷄尾腸、蝦、青瓜順序穿起，排在塗油燒熱之鐵板上兩邊各烤 1 分鐘。上桌時淋下汁料即可食用。

Seafood in Mustard Sauce

涼 拌 三 鮮

Ingredients:

4 oz (112 g) canned abalones
4 oz (112 g) medium size prawns
4 oz (112 g) squids
1 tbsp ginger juice
a pinch of pepper
2 cups water
1 oz (28 g) agar agar
3 cups warm water

Condiment Mix-
2 tbsp light soy
1 tbsp sugar
2 tbsp French mustard
1 tsp chicken powder
1 tbsp abalone's stock
4 tbsp mayonnaise

Method:

* Remove the abalones from the can and keep the stock for later use. Take out 4 oz (112 g) of the abalones and slice into thin pieces. Put the remaining abalones in a plastic box to keep in the refrigerator for other usage.
* Shell, devein and slit the back of the prawns. Wash under the running tap and dry with a towel. Put the prawns on a platter for later use.
* Wash, skin, dry and make a crisscross pattern on the inside of the squids. Cut into thin pieces. Put on a platter together with the prawns and marinate with the ginger juice and pepper for 20 minutes.
* Put the water in a saucepan and bring it to boil. Cook the prawns and squids for about 40 to 60 seconds. Remove and leave to cool.
* Soak the agar agar in the warm water for 30 minutes then cut into 2″ (5 cm) lengths. Squeeze out the excess water and place on a platter. Arrange the abalones, prawns and squids on top of the agar agar and serve cold immediately.
* Stir the condiment mix thoroughly in a small bowl then pour over the seafood. Mix well before eating.

材料：

罐頭鮑魚 4 安（112克）
中蝦 4 安（112克）
鮮魷 4 安（112克）
羌汁 1 湯匙
古月粉少許
大菜 1 安（28克）

調味 —
生抽 2 湯匙
糖 1 湯匙
芥醬 2 湯匙
鷄粉 1 茶匙
鮑魚湯 1 湯匙
沙律醬 4 湯匙

製法：

* 鮑魚從罐中取出，將湯汁留作上湯用，取出 4 安（112克）切片，剩下來的放在膠合內。置冰箱中留爲別用。
* 蝦去壳挑腸從背部以刀介開，放在水喉下冲洗乾淨，以毛巾吸乾水份，放在深碟上候用。
* 鮮魷清除內臟撕去皮洗淨，在內介花紋切件。與蝦同放碟中，加入羌汁及古月粉醃20分鐘。
* 鍋中放水 2 杯煮沸，將蝦及魷魚件放入迅速煮至捲起，約需40至60秒鐘。取出隔去水份攤凍。
* 大菜洗淨以暖水浸半小時剪成 2 吋（5 公分）段，揸乾水份後攤放在碟中。鮑魚、蝦及魷魚放在大菜上面即可上桌。
* 調味料放於小碗中和勻，淋在海鮮上拌勻食用。

Shrimp and Egg Patties
煎 蝦 餅

Shrimp and Egg Patties
煎 蝦 餅

Ingredients:

10 oz (280 g) shelled shrimps
1 tbsp salt
1 tbsp cornflour
1 tbsp chopped parsley
1 tsp chopped spring onions
3 eggs
a few tbsp oil for shallow frying
a few parsley sprigs for garnishing

Seasoning-
½ tsp salt
½ tsp sugar
a pinch of pepper
1 tsp cornflour
1 tsp sesame oil

Method:

* Devein and toss the shrimps with the salt and cornflour then rinse under a running tap till the water runs clear. Pat dry with a clean towel and dice. Season with half of the above seasoning. Place on to a platter with the parsley and spring onions.
* Break the eggs into a mixing bowl and stir in the remaining seasoning. Slide in the shrimps, parsley and spring onions and whisk until evenly mixed.
* Heat a pan with 2 tbsp of oil.

Put a tbsp of batter in the boiling oil to shallow fry till both sides are golden. Repeat, remove and dish. Garnish with the parsley sprigs.

材料：

蝦仁10安（280克）
芫茜葉 1 湯匙
葱粒 1 茶匙
鷄蛋 3 隻
油數湯匙煎蝦餅
芫茜裝飾

調味 —
鹽 ½ 茶匙
糖 ½ 茶匙
古月粉少許
生粉 1 茶匙
蔴油 1 茶匙

製法：

* 蝦仁挑腸後放脊箕內加鹽及生粉各 1 湯匙拌勻。放水喉下冲洗乾淨，用毛巾吸乾水份切成幼粒。用二分一調味料略撈後，放碟中加芫茜、葱粒和勻。
* 蛋打在大碗中，加入其餘調味料，試妥味後與蝦粒、芫茜、葱等一同打勻。
* 鑊燒熱放下油 2 湯匙煮沸。將蝦蛋混合物逐湯匙放入鑊中煎至兩邊呈金黃色。以碟盛起上桌。

1. This is Eugene's first attempt in the kitchen, understandably he is filled with apprehension.

2. After a while, he starts to enjoy himself.

3. Grace adds the shrimps to the beaten eggs.

4. Together they begin the shallow-frying process.

5. Eugene is having so much fun that he forgets that Grace is there too.

6. Eventually Grace has the chance to try out her skill.

7. Eugene stands by to advise Grace like a real professional!

8. They cannot contain their excitement over their success.

Steamed Fish Slices with Preserved Prunes

梅 子 蒸 魚 腩

Ingredients:

½ lb (224 g) fish fillet
½ oz (14 g) preserved ginger
½ oz (14 g) preserved pickles
½ oz (14 g) preserved prunes
2 slices ginger
2 garlic cloves

2 spring onions
1 parsley sprig
1 tbsp shredded chillies

Fish Marinade-
2 tbsp ginger juice
½ tsp pepper

Seasoning-
1 ½ tbsp ground bean paste
1 ½ tbsp light soy
1 ½ tbsp sugar
a pinch of pepper
2 tbsp oil

Method:

* Wipe and slice the fish fillet into ¼″ (0.6 cm) thick pieces. Marinate with the ginger juice and pepper for 10 minutes.
* Shred the preserved ginger and pickles. Deseed the preserved prunes. Mince the ginger and garlic. Shred the spring onions. Wash and trim the parsley. Mix the seasoning with the minced ginger, garlic and prunes evenly. Season to taste and pour over the fish slices to stir well.
* Transfer the fish to another platter and mix in half of the shredded chillies. Place in a steamer and cover tightly then steam over a wok of boiling water for 8 minutes and remove.
* Scatter the shredded spring onions, parsley and chillies on top of the dish and serve hot at once.

材料：

鱸魚腩½磅（224克） 醃魚料—
酸羌½安（14克） 羌汁2湯匙
酸蕎頭½安（14克） 古月粉½茶匙
酸梅½安（14克）
羌2片
蒜頭2粒
葱2條
芫茜1棵
紅椒絲1湯匙

調味—
磨豉1½湯匙
生抽1½湯匙
糖1½湯匙
古月粉少許
油2湯匙

製法：

* 將班腩去鱗洗淨抹乾，切件。用羌汁及古月粉醃10分鐘。
* 酸羌，蕎頭切絲，酸梅去核搗爛，羌、蒜頭剁爛成茸。葱切絲，芫茜摘妥。調味料和勻後與羌、蒜茸及梅子醬混合，倒在魚腩上撈勻，試妥味。
* 將魚腩轉放另一碟中，灑上紅椒絲數條，置密蓋蒸籠內架在沸水鑊中蒸8分鐘，取出。
* 葱絲、芫茜葉及紅椒絲灑在魚上面，即可上桌。

Stuffed Tomatoes
with Shrimps
番 茄 沙 律 蝦

Ingredients:

4 oz (112 g) cooked shrimps
a shake of pepper
1 oz (28 g) pears
   or water chestnuts
1 oz (28 g) celery
1 hard boiled egg
½ oz (14 g) sweet peas
½ oz (14 g) sweetcorn
1 cup boiling salted water
12 tomatoes

Seasoning-
2 tbsp mayonnaise
2 tbsp tomato ketchup
1 tsp hot broadbean paste

Method:

* Shell and dust the shrimps with pepper. Peel and dice the water chestnuts, celery and egg.
* Blanch the peas and sweetcorn in the boiling salted water. Refresh and drain. Put the shrimps and all the diced ingredients in a clean mixing bowl.
* Cream the seasoning in a bowl and mix thoroughly. Add to the mixed ingredients to bind well. Chill in the refrigerator for 1 hour.
* Wash and dry the tomatoes. Slice off the tops of the tomatoes and scoop out the flesh. Use the tops as lids and discard or reserve the flesh for other dishes.
* Dry the inside of the tomatoes with kitchen paper, then stuff each one with the mixed ingredients. Chill the stuffed tomatoes in the refrigerator for 1 hour. Arrange on a platter and serve cold.

材料：

熟蝦 4 安（112克）
古月粉少許
啤梨或馬蹄 1 安（28克）
西芹 1 安（28克）
熟蛋 1 隻
青豆 ½ 安（14克）
粟米 ½ 安（14克）
沸鹽水 1 杯
番茄12隻

調味 —
沙律醬 2 湯匙
茄汁 2 湯匙
豆瓣醬 1 茶匙

製法：

* 熟蝦去壳以古月粉拌勻。啤梨、西芹、熟蛋切粒。
* 青豆、粟米放沸鹽水中飛水過冷河。隔乾水份。深盆洗淨抹乾，將蝦及各粒放入。
* 小碗 1 隻將調味料傾入攪拌至均勻。加入深盆內與各料撈勻，置雪柜中雪 1 小時。
* 番茄洗淨抹乾，在頂部切去約 ⅓ 份。（可用以作蓋）將茄肉挖出與茄蓋一同留為別用。
* 番茄倒轉流去水份再用布抹乾，取出已雪凍之沙律蝦，釀在番茄內，排放在碟上即可上桌。

Braised Quails' Eggs
with Mushrooms

白菌燴鵪蛋

Ingredients:

5 oz (140 g) fresh mushrooms
4 cups water
20 quails' eggs
2 cups spicy sauce
2 oz (56 g) carrots
1 cup boiling water
2 oz (56 g) green vegetables
1 tsp salt

1 tsp sugar
1 tbsp oil
1 slice ginger
1 shallot
2 tbsp oil

Seasoning-
¼ cup water
¼ cup spicy sauce
1 tsp light soy

½ tsp sugar
a pinch of pepper

Gravy Mix -
1 tsp cornflour
1 tbsp water
½ tsp dark soy
½ tsp sesame oil

Method:

* Wash, trim and quarter the mushrooms.
* Pour the water in a 2-quart saucepan then add the quails' eggs and bring to boil over low heat. Continue to boil for 2 minutes. Remove and soak in cold water for 30 minutes. Shell and transfer the quails' eggs into the warm spicy sauce and leave to soak for 1 hour. Remove and drain.
* Peel and slice the carrots into $\frac{1}{8}''$ (3 mm) thick pieces. Cut a pattern with a vegetable cutter then immerse in the boiling water for 1 hour.
* Wash and trim the green vegetables. Blanch in the same boiling water with the salt, sugar and oil. Remove and drain. Arrange on a platter.
* Shred the ginger and slice the shallot.
* Place a frying pan over low heat and bring the oil to the boil. Stir in the ginger and shallot to sauté till fragrant. Add the eggs, mushrooms and carrots to mix well. Pour in the seasoning to braise for 1 minute. Thicken the sauce with the gravy mix. Drop in the sesame oil and dish.

材料：

鮮白菌5安（140克）
鵪鶉蛋20隻
鹵水2杯
甘筍2安（56克）
白菜數棵
羌1片
葱頭1粒
油2湯匙起鑊

調味 —
水¼杯
鹵水¼杯
生抽1茶匙
糖½茶匙
古月粉少許

饆汁—
生粉1茶匙
水1湯匙
老抽½茶匙
蔴油½茶匙

製法：

* 白菌洗乾淨，每粒分切四份候用。
* 鵪鶉蛋放凍水中煮5至6分鐘，浸凍後去殼放在暖鹵水中浸1小時，撈起隔乾水份。
* 甘筍切花飛水，浸於沸水中1小時。
* 白菜摘妥洗淨，放1杯沸水中加鹽、糖各1茶匙；油1湯匙同煮片刻取出隔去水份排放碟中。
* 羌切絲，葱頭切片。
* 燒熱煎鑊，將油煮沸，爆香羌葱片。傾入白菌、鶉蛋及甘筍同炒片刻。倒下調味料煮沸再將饆料和勻慢慢加入，最後洒蔴油即可上碟。

Egg Puffs in Hot Sauce
魚 香 烘 蛋

Ingredients:

5 large eggs
½ tsp salt
4 tbsp oil
1 tbsp trimmed parsley
1 tbsp shredded spring onion

Sauce-
1 tbsp diced spring onions

1 tsp minced ginger
1 tbsp diced pears
1 tsp minced garlic
¾ tbsp hot broadbean paste
2 tsp soy sauce
1 ½ tsp sugar
1 tsp vinegar
1 tsp sesame oil
½ cup stock

Gravy Mix -
1 tsp cornflour
1 tbsp water
¼ tsp dark soy

Method:

* Shell the eggs and add the salt and 2 tbsp of the oil to beat together thoroughly in a mixing bowl.
* Heat an 8″ (20 cm) frying pan and bring the remaining 2 tbsp oil to boil. Pour in the beaten eggs to shallow fry for 2 to 3 minutes till the batter puffs up. Turn over and cook for a further 2 minutes, until both sides are golden brown. Turn out on to a chopping board and cut into 12 small triangles, then arrange on a platter.
* Put all the sauce ingredients into a bowl and mix well. Pour into a saucepan and bring to the boil.
* Slowly add the gravy mixture to thicken the sauce. Adjust the seasoning to taste and pour over the egg puffs. Garnish with parsley and spring onion. Serve hot.

材料：

大鷄蛋 5 隻
鹽 ½ 茶匙
油 4 湯匙
芫茜葉 1 湯匙
葱絲 1 湯匙

魚香汁－
葱粒 1 湯匙
羗茸 1 茶匙
啤梨茸 1 湯匙
蒜茸 1 茶匙
豆瓣醬 ¾ 湯匙
生抽 2 茶匙
糖 1½ 茶匙
醋 1 茶匙
蔴油 1 茶匙
上湯 ½ 杯

饙汁－
生粉 1 茶匙
水 1 湯匙
老抽 ¼ 茶匙

製法：

* 鷄蛋去壳放碗內加鹽及油 2 湯匙打勻。
* 燒紅 8 吋平底鑊加餘油 2 湯匙煮沸，隨將蛋液倒下慢火煎烘約 2 至 3 分鐘。反轉再煎 2 分鐘至兩面金黃色。倒出在砧板上切成 12 份小三角形，排放在碟上。
* 魚香汁料放小碗中拌勻，倒入鍋內煮沸。
* 饙料以小匙拌勻後，慢慢流入魚香汁和成半稀杰之饙汁。試妥味後淋在蛋上。可用芫茜葉及葱絲裝飾上桌。

Shallow Fried Egg Sheets
煎 蛋 皮

Ingredients:

3 medium size eggs
½ tsp salt
¹/₈ tsp pepper
2 tbsp oil
2 tsp sesame oil

Method:

* Wash and towel dry the eggs. Break the shells against the edge of the mixing bowl. Drop the eggs into the bowl.
* Sprinkle the salt and pepper on the eggs then whisk thoroughly with a pair of wooden chopsticks. Gradually beat in the oil to mix well.
* Heat the frying pan on the stove over low heat then use a brush to grease the pan with some sesame oil. Pour in one quarter of the egg batter and swirl the pan till the base is entirely covered with the batter. Continue to shallow fry over low heat until the batter has solidified.
* Separate the egg sheet from the pan with a blunt knife and quickly flip the pan upside down to turn the egg sheet on a platter. Leave to cool before use. Repeat 3 times to finish the batter. The batter should make 4 egg sheets in total.

1. Grease the pan with oil.

材料：

鷄蛋 3 隻
鹽 $\frac{1}{2}$ 茶匙
胡椒粉 $\frac{1}{8}$ 茶匙
油 2 湯匙
蔴油 2 茶匙

製法：

* 鷄蛋洗淨抹乾，在碗邊將蛋殼敲破，將蛋液傾在深碗中。
* 鹽與胡椒粉灑在蛋上，以木筷打約20下，跟着逐少將油加入打至完全混成一體。
* 平底煎鍋放在爐上慢火燒熱，以毛筆將蔴油塗在煎鍋上，即把 $\frac{1}{4}$ 蛋液傾下搪勻至完全蓋住鍋底為止。用文火煎約 1 分鐘至蛋液完全凝結時即可以小餐刀從鍋邊揭起小許。然後倒在砧板上攤凍用。
* 重複 3 次，直至全部蛋液煎完。共得蛋皮 4 張。

2. Shallow-fry the batter until it has solidified.

3. Remove the egg sheet from the pan with a knife.

Sweetcorn and Egg Chowder

粟 米 蛋 花 羹

Ingredients:

2 eggs
2 cups creamy sweetcorn
4 cups water
1 spring onion
2 tbsp oil
1 slice ginger

Seasoning-
½ tsp wine
1½ tsp salt
½ tsp chicken essence
1 tsp sugar
a pinch of pepper
2 tbsp cornflour
3 tbsp stock
1 tsp sesame oil

Method:

* Break the eggs and separate the yolks from the whites then place in 2 separate bowls. Beat both the yolks and the whites thoroughly.
* Place the sweetcorn in a bowl and stir in 1 cup of water then leave aside.
* Wash and dice the spring onion.
* Heat a clean earthenware pot or stainless steel saucepan over moderate heat. Add the oil to sauté the ginger and discard. Sizzle the wine and pour in the remaining water to bring to boil. Stir in the sweetcorn mixture, then season with the salt, chicken essence, sugar and pepper. Mix the cornflour with the stock and trickle into the boiling soup, stirring constantly. Add the egg yolks, then the egg whites, gradually. Scoop into serving bowls and sprinkle the sesame oil and spring onion on top. Serve hot.

材料：

鷄蛋 2 隻
罐頭粟米 2 杯
水 4 杯
葱 1 棵
油 2 湯匙
羗 1 片

調味一
酒 ½ 茶匙
鹽 1½ 茶匙
鷄精 ½ 茶匙
糖 1 茶匙
古月粉少許
生粉 2 湯匙
上湯或水 3 湯匙
蔴油 1 茶匙

製法：

* 鷄蛋分黃別白，以兩個小碗分別盛開後略打。
* 粟米以深碗盛起，用水 1 杯拌散，置一旁候用。
* 葱洗淨切粒。
* 瓦鍋或不銹鋼保洗淨置中火爐上燒熱。將油流入煮沸，炸香羗片棄去。贊酒倒入其餘 3 杯水煮沸。即下已拌散之粟米糊，不斷以木匙攪動。跟着將鹽、鷄精、糖及古月粉拌入。待重沸時，將生粉與上湯混和慢慢加入拌勻。最後將蛋黃蛋白分別慢慢流入以筷子攪成絲，盛在湯碗內，上灑蔴油及葱，即可食用。

Blanched Leeks in Soy Sauce

白 灼 韭 菜 心

Ingredients:

1 lb (½ kg) green leeks
2 shallots
1 slice ginger
3 cups water
2 tsp salt
4 tbsp oil

Seasoning-
3 tbsp light soy
2 tbsp sugar
a pinch of black pepper

Method:

* Clean and cut off one third of the leeks, retaining two-third of the most tender part.
* Peel and slice the shallots. Shred the ginger.
* Heat a frying pan on the stove and pour in the water and salt to bring to boil. Drop in half of the above oil then slide in the leeks to blanch for 10 seconds. Remove and drain. Section into 1½″ (4 cm) lengths and arrange on a platter.
* Clean and heat a small pan with the remaining oil. Sauté the shallots and ginger till light brown. Pour in the light soy, sugar and pepper and bring to the boil. Turn off the heat and spoon over the leeks and serve.

材料：

韮菜心1磅（½公斤）
葱頭2粒
羗1片
水3杯
鹽2茶匙
油4湯匙

調味一
生抽3湯匙
糖2湯匙
黑胡椒粉少許

製法：

* 韮菜心洗淨，將約三份一之硬莖切去棄之。只留全棵約三份之二最嫩部份。
* 葱頭去衣切片。羗切絲。
* 煎鍋一個，放在爐上燒熱。將水與鹽加入煮沸。隨將一半油倒下，即將韮菜心滑下灼約10秒鐘。取出隔清水份，切成約1½吋（4公分）度。排在長碟上。
* 小煎鍋一個，洗淨重燒熱，把餘下之油煮沸。加入葱、羗絲炸至微黃色。跟着將調味料傾入煮滾。熄去爐火，淋在韮菜心上即可上桌。

Chilled Beanthread with Cucumber and Ham

涼 拌 粉 絲

Ingredients:

4 oz (112 g) beanthread
3 cups water
4 oz (112 g) cucumber
4 oz (112 g) ham
2 eggs
2 parsley sprigs (optional)
1 tsp oil

Egg Seasoning-
¼ tsp salt
⅛ tsp pepper
1 tbsp oil

Condiment Mix-
2 tbsp light soy
1 tbsp sugar
2 tbsp vinegar
½ tsp chicken powder
1 tbsp sesame oil
½ tsp minced garlic (optional)

Method:

* Cut the beanthread into 2" (5 cm) lengths and soak in a few cups of water for 30 minutes then drain.
* Bring the above water to boil, put in the beanthread and turn off the heat immediately. Leave to soak for 5 minutes. Drain in a colander and wash under a running tap. Drain again and arrange on to a platter.
* Wash and shred the cucumber into similar lengths to the beanthread. Place the shredded cucumber on one side of the platter on top of the beanthread.
* Shred the ham into similar size to the beanthread and place in the middle, next to the cucumber on top of the beanthread.
* Shell the eggs and beat well with the seasoning. Wash and trim the parsley.
* Heat a pan and brush with the oil. Pour in half of the beaten eggs and swirl to cover the bottom of the pan. Heat gently until the eggs set to form an egg sheet. Remove on to a chopping board and leave it to cool. Roll it up into a 2" (5 cm) cylinder and shred thinly. Arrange beside the shredded ham. Repeat the process with the remaining half of the beaten eggs.
* Chill the shredded ingredients in the refrigerator for 20 minutes.
* Prepare the condiment mix in a small bowl. Stir in the parsley to mix well. Pour the mixture over the shredded ingredients before serving.

材料：

粉絲 4 安（112克）
水 3 杯
青瓜 4 安（112克）
火腿 4 安（112克）
蛋 2 隻
芫茜 2 棵
油 1 茶匙

蛋調味 —
鹽 ¼ 茶匙
胡椒粉 ⅛ 茶匙
油 1 湯匙

汁料 —
生抽 2 湯匙
糖 1 湯匙
浙醋 2 湯匙
鷄粉 ½ 茶匙
蔴油 1 湯匙
蒜茸 ½ 茶匙（隨意）

製法：

* 粉絲剪成約 2 吋（ 5 公分）段，以水浸 ½ 小時，倒起隔去水份。
* 水 3 杯煮沸將粉絲加入隨即停火浸 5 分鐘以筲箕盛起放水喉下沖凍，隔乾後放在碟上。
* 青瓜洗淨切長度與粉絲相等之幼絲，排放在粉絲一旁上。
* 火腿亦切長度相等之幼絲，排在粉絲中央。
* 蛋去壳加調味打勻。芫茜洗淨摘妥。
* 煎鍋燒熱以毛筆掃上油，將一半蛋液倒下搪開煎成蛋皮。揭起放在砧板上攤凍，捲成長筒再切幼絲，排放在火腿旁邊，另一半蛋液同樣製成蛋絲加上。放雪柜中雪20分鐘。
* 將汁料全放在碗內加芫茜葉和勻倒在各絲上，拌勻食用。

Chinese Cabbage with
Minced Garlic
蒜茸白菜仔

Ingredients:

1 lb (½ kg) Chinese cabbage
3 garlic cloves
1 slice ginger
2 tbsp oil

Seasoning-
1 tsp salt
¼ tsp sugar
½ tsp sesame oil

Method:

* Wash, trim and drain the cabbage.
* Mince the garlic and ginger finely.
* Heat the wok and bring the oil to boil. Sauté the minced garlic and ginger till fragrant. Pour in the cabbage and salt to stir fry briskly for a few seconds then add the remaining seasoning to mix well. Remove and dish.

材料：

白菜仔1磅（½公斤）
蒜頭3粒
羌1片
油2湯匙

調味一
鹽1茶匙
糖¼茶匙
蔴油½茶匙

製法：

* 白菜用清水洗淨摘妥以箐箕隔乾水份。
* 蒜頭剁茸、羌亦剁茸。
* 燒紅鑊加油煮沸傾下蒜、羌茸及鹽爆香。將菜仔倒入迅速翻炒十數下。加入其餘調味料兜勻即可上碟。

Sautéed Cucumber with Ham

火 腿 拌 絲 瓜

Ingredients:

1 lb (½ kg) cucumber (chinese)
4 oz (112 g) ham
1 slice ginger
1 shallot
2 spring onions
2 tbsp oil

Seasoning-
½ tsp salt
1 tsp sugar
1 tsp wine
2 tbsp water
a pinch of pepper
1 tsp sesame oil

Method:

* Wash and peel the cucumber. Cut lengthwise into halves. Core and cut into 1"x 1½" (2.5 cm x 4 cm) thick slices.
* Cut the ham into bite-sized pieces or diamond shape. Leave aside for later use.
* Sliver the ginger. Slice the shallot. Section the spring onions.
* Heat the wok to bring the oil to boil. Saute the ginger and shallot until aromatic. Put in the cucumber with the salt and sugar to stir fry for 20 seconds. Sizzle the wine, add the water and pepper to toss well. Turn off the heat and pour in the ham and spring onions. Sprinkle the sesame oil to mix well and dish.

材料：

絲瓜 1 磅（½ 公斤）
火腿 4 安（112克）
羌 1 片
葱頭 1 粒
葱 2 條
油 2 湯匙

調味一
鹽 ½ 茶匙
糖 1 茶匙
酒 1 茶匙
水 2 湯匙
古月粉少許
蔴油 1 茶匙

製法：

* 絲瓜洗淨間疏去皮，剖開兩邊，割去瓜囊。切成 1 吋×1½ 吋（2½ 公分× 4 公分）之骨牌片。
* 火腿切骨牌或菱形，放置一旁候用。
* 羌片成小薄片。葱頭切片，葱切段。
* 燒紅鑊加油煮沸，放下羌，葱頭片爆香。隨將絲瓜倒入鑊中，加鹽糖略炒。贊酒將水及古月粉加入兜勻。停火傾入火腿片及葱度，灑蔴油拌勻即可上碟。

Winter Melon Soup
冬 瓜 粒 湯

Ingredients:

10 oz (280 g) winter melon
2 oz (56 g) ham
2 oz (56 g) shelled shrimps
a pinch of pepper
2 oz (56 g) button mushrooms
3 cooked Chinese mushrooms
3 cups water

Seasoning-
¾ tsp salt
½ tsp sugar
¼ tsp chicken essence
½ tsp sesame oil to sprinkle on top

Method:

* Peel and wash the winter melon. Dice into ⅓″ (1 cm) cubes.
* Dice the ham into cubes of similar size to the melon.
* Coat the shrimps with pepper. Dice both kinds of mushrooms.
* Fill an earthenware pot or stainless steel saucepan with the water and bring to boil over moderate heat. Reduce the heat and add the diced melon and mushrooms to simmer for 8 minutes. Season to taste and stir in the remaining ingredients. Continue to boil for 2 minutes. Scoop into a soup tureen and sprinkle the sesame oil on top. Serve hot.

材料：

冬瓜10安（280克）
火腿 2 安（56克）
熟蝦肉 2 安（56克）
胡椒粉少許
白菌 2 安（56克）
熟冬菇 3 隻
水 3 杯

調味一
鹽 ¾ 茶匙
糖 ½ 茶匙
鷄精 ¼ 茶匙
蔴油 ½ 茶匙灑面

製法：

* 冬瓜去皮洗淨切成 ⅓ 吋（1 公分）丁方粒。
* 火腿亦切同樣大小丁方粒。熟蝦用古月粉略撈。白菌與熟冬菇皆切粒候用。
* 將水注入瓦鍋或不銹鋼保內，放在中火爐上加冬瓜粒及冬菇煮沸。轉用文火煮約 8 分鐘，即將調味料及其他各粒傾入再煮 2 分鐘，盛在湯碗內灑蔴油上桌。

Yam in Hot Tomato Sauce

串 燒 芋 仔

Ingredients:

1 lb (½ kg) yams
4 cups water
½ tbsp salt
1 tsp sugar
½ oz (14 g) bacon
½ oz (14 g) celery
½ oz (14 g) water chestnuts
  or pears
½ oz (14 g) onions
1 garlic clove
2 tbsp oil
1 tbsp chopped spring onions

Condiment Mix-
3 tbsp tomato ketchup
1 tbsp broadbean paste
2 tbsp light soy
1 tsp chicken powder
1 tbsp sugar
1 tbsp sesame oil

Method:

* Wash the yams and place them in a saucepan. Next add the water, salt and sugar and boil for 15 minutes. Remove from the stove and leave to cool. Peel and cut each yam in half. Thread the yams onto the skewers.
* Mince the bacon. Wash, trim and mince the celery and water chestnuts. Peel and mince the onions.
* Place all the minced ingredients in a bowl and stir in the condiment mix. Mince the garlic.
* Heat a small frying pan with the oil to sauté the minced garlic. Stir in the condiment mix and simmer for a few seconds. Turn off the heat.
* Arrange the yam kebabs on a heated iron plate and grill each side for about 1 minute. Pour the hot sauce on top then sprinkle with the chopped spring onions.

材料：

芋仔1磅（½公斤）
水 4 杯
鹽½湯匙
糖 1 茶匙
烟肉½安（14克）
芹菜½安（14克）
馬蹄或啤梨½安（14克）
洋葱½安（14克）
蒜頭1粒
油 2 湯匙
葱粒 1 湯匙

汁料一
番茄醬 3 湯匙
豆瓣醬 1 湯匙
生抽 2 湯匙
鷄粉 1 茶匙
糖 1 湯匙
蔴油 1 湯匙

製法：

* 芋仔洗淨放在深煲內加水及鹽糖煮約15分鐘，取出攤凍撕去皮，每個分切成 2 等份，以長針或竹籤插成一串。
* 烟肉切成茸，芹菜洗淨切幼。馬蹄或啤梨去皮切幼。洋葱去衣剁茸。
* 用深碗將以上各茸盛起，加入汁料拌匀。蒜頭去衣剁茸。
* 小鍋1個燒熱，將油傾入煮沸，爆香蒜茸後加入已拌匀之混合料煮片刻停火。
* 芋仔排在已燒熱之鐵板上，兩邊略煎後將汁料全部贊下上碟，灑葱粒裝飾。

Cold Noodles with Peanut Sauce

雙　絲　冷　麵

Ingredients:

10 oz (280 g) cold or oiled noodles
1 tbsp cooked oil
2 oz (56 g) ham
2 oz (56 g) cooked chicken meat
2 cooked mushrooms

2 oz (56 g) red cabbage
2 oz (56 g) cabbage
2 oz (56 g) cucumber
1 oz (28 g) carrots
2 tbsp oil
¼ tsp salt
2 tbsp sesame seeds

Seasoning-
1⅓ tbsp sugar
2 tbsp light soy
2 to 3 tbsp stock
2 tbsp peanut butter
1 tsp sesame oil
½ tsp chilli oil
a pinch of pepper

Method:

* Wash the noodles with warm water and drain. Coat the noodles with the cooked oil then leave on a platter for later use.
* Shred the ham, chicken and mushrooms.
* Wash and shred both kinds of cabbage, the cucumber and carrots.
* Heat the wok or pan with the oil to sauté all the shredded ingredients. Sprinkle the salt to stir thoroughly. Turn off the heat and mix in the cold noodles. Chill in the refrigerator for 1 hour.
* Mix all the seasoning together in a bowl. Season to taste and pour over the noodles.
* Wash, parch then scatter the sesame seeds on the noodles and serve.

材料：

冷麵10安（280克）
熟油 1 湯匙
火腿 2 安（56克）
熟鷄肉 2 安（56克）
熟冬菇 2 隻
紅椰菜 2 安（56克）
白椰菜 2 安（56克）
靑瓜 2 安（56克）
甘笋 1 安（28克）
油 2 湯匙
鹽¼茶匙
芝蔴 2 湯匙

調味－
糖1⅓湯匙
生抽 2 湯匙
上湯 2 至 3 湯匙
花生醬 2 湯匙
蔴油 1 茶匙
辣油½茶匙
古月粉少許

製法：

* 冷麵以暖水洗淨隔乾水份，再以油撈勻放碟中候用。
* 火腿、熟鷄肉、冬菇皆切絲。
* 紅椰菜、白椰菜、靑瓜、甘笋全部洗淨切絲候用。
* 燒紅鑊加油煮沸爆香各絲加鹽炒勻。停火將冷麵傾入拌勻上碟，放雪柜中雪 1 小時。
* 調味料放碗中和勻試妥味，淋在冷麵上。食時再撈勻。
* 芝蔴洗淨放在燒熱之白鑊烙香，灑在冷麵上。

Congee with Sliced Beef and Egg

窩 蛋 牛 肉 粥

Ingredients:

¼ cup rice
½ tbsp oil
½ tsp salt
1 beancurd sheet (optional)
10 ginkgo nuts (optional)

8 to 9 cups water
4 oz (112 g) beef
1 spring onion
1 parsley sprig
1 egg
1 tbsp shredded ginger

Beef Marinade-
1½ tsp light soy
¾ tsp sugar
½ tsp wine
a pinch of pepper
1 tsp cornflour
¼ cup water
1 tbsp oil, to be added last

Seasoning-
1 tsp salt
a pinch of pepper
1 tsp sesame oil

Method:

* Wash and drain the rice in a sieve. Mix well with the oil and salt.
* Wash and break the beancurd sheet into small pieces. Shell and peel the ginkgo nuts.
* Bring the water to boil in a deep saucepan. Add the rice, beancurd sheet and ginkgo nuts to simmer over low heat for 1½ hours. Season to taste.
* Wash and slice the beef. Immerse in the mixed marinade for 30 minutes. Blend in the oil to marinate for a further 30 minutes.
* Wash and shred the spring onion. Clean and trim the parsley.
* Reboil the congee and put in the beef. Turn off the heat and stir evenly. Pour into a soup tureen and break an egg on top of the congee. Sprinkle with the spring onion, parsley and ginger. Serve hot.

材料：

米 $\frac{1}{4}$ 杯
油 $\frac{1}{2}$ 湯匙
鹽 $\frac{1}{2}$ 茶匙
腐皮 1 塊（隨意）
白果 10 粒（隨意）
水 8 至 9 杯
牛肉 4 安（112 克）
葱 1 棵
芫茜 1 棵
蛋 1 隻
羌絲 1 湯匙

醃肉料一
生抽 1 $\frac{1}{2}$ 茶匙
糖 $\frac{3}{4}$ 茶匙
酒 $\frac{1}{2}$ 茶匙
古月粉少許
生粉 1 茶匙
水 $\frac{1}{4}$ 杯
油 1 湯匙（後下）

調味一
鹽 1 茶匙
古月粉少許
蔴油 1 茶匙

製法：

* 米洗淨放在篩中隔乾水份，用油、鹽拌勻。
* 腐皮洗淨撕碎。白果去壳去衣。
* 將水放入深鍋內以中火煮沸。加入米、腐皮、白果後改用文火煮約 1 $\frac{1}{2}$ 小時，加調味試妥味。
* 牛肉洗淨切片，放入已拌勻之醃料中醃 30 分鐘。加油再醃 $\frac{1}{2}$ 小時。
* 葱洗淨切絲，芫茜洗淨摘妥。
* 將粥煮至再滾時，即將牛肉放入立刻熄去爐火拌勻；以大湯兜盛起，鷄蛋去壳放在中央。灑上葱絲、芫茜、羌絲即成，食時將蛋撈勻。

Instant Noodles with Shredded Ham
腿 絲 即 食 麵

Ingredients:

3 cups boiling water
2 packets instant noodles (200 g)
3 oz (84 g) ham
½ cup tinned mushrooms
2 spring onions
2 shallots
2 tbsp oil

Seasoning-
½ cup water
¼ tsp salt
¼ tsp chicken powder
1 tbsp light soy
2 tsp sugar
1 tsp sesame oil, to be added last

Method:

* Half fill a saucepan with boiling water. Slide in the instant noodles to blanch for about 1 minute. Loosen the noodles with a pair of chopsticks. Remove and drain.
* Shred the ham and slice the mushrooms. Wash and section the spring onions. Peel and slice the shallots.
* Heat the frying pan with the oil and bring it to boil. Sauté the sliced shallots. Mix the seasoning (except the sesame oil) evenly and pour into the pan. Add the blanched noodles to braise for half a minute till the stock is absorbed by the noodles. Stir in the shredded ham, mushrooms and sectioned spring onions. Turn off the heat then sprinkle the sesame oil on top. Dish and serve.

材料：

即食麵 2 包（200克）
火腿 3 安（84克）
罐頭白菌 ½ 杯
葱 2 棵
葱頭 2 粒
油 2 湯匙

調味—
水 ½ 杯
鹽 ¼ 茶匙
鷄粉 ¼ 茶匙
生抽 1 湯匙
糖 2 茶匙
蔴油 1 茶匙（後下）

製法：

* 預備沸水半鍋，將即食麵放入以筷子挑崧煮軟。約需 1 分鐘即成。取出隔去水份候用。
* 火腿切絲，白菌切片，葱洗淨切度，葱頭去衣切片。
* 煎鍋燒熱，將油傾下煮沸，炸香葱頭片。即將水與調味料拌勻加入。待重沸時將已飛水之麵條倒入煮 ½ 分鐘。至吸透味後，把火腿絲及白菌片葱度一同拌入捞勻。停火灑蔴油和勻即可上碟。

Rice with Oil and Salt

油 鹽 飯

Ingredients:

2 cups rice
2 tbsp oil
1 tbsp salt
2¼ to 2½ cups water

Method:

* Wash and drain the rice in a sieve.
* Pour the rice into a casserole or saucepan and mix in the oil and

salt. Add the water and cover the casserole. Place over moderate heat for approximately 6 minutes to bring the water to boil. Lower the heat and continue to cook for 12 minutes. Turn off the heat and leave to mature on the hot stove for another 15 minutes. Remove the lid then loosen the rice with a pair of chopsticks. Serve hot or leave it to cool and stir fry with other ingredients.

N.B. The measurement of water for cooking rice depends largely on the type of rice used. In general, more water is required for cooking long grain rice and less for short grain rice. Only long grain rice can be used for fried rice dishes.

The ratio of water to rice for long grain (fried) rice ranges from 1:1 to 1:1⅛. Use this ratio for each cup of rice. The ratio for plain steamed rice is about 1:1⅕ to 1:1¼. Use 1⅕ to 1¼ cups of water for every cup of rice.

You should always test the water requirement when you start to use a new brand of rice.

材料：

米 2 杯
油 2 湯匙
鹽 1 湯匙
水2¼至2½杯

製法：

＊ 米洗淨，放在篩內隔乾水份。
＊ 瓦鍋或不銹鋼煲或電飯煲一個。將米倒入，加油、鹽與米一同拌勻後，把水注入。蓋上鍋蓋以中火煮約 6 分鐘至沸。轉用文火續煮12分鐘，將火熄掉留在爐上利用餘溫焗約15分鐘。即可揭蓋以筷子將飯挑鬆後取用。

＊註：
煮飯之用水量通常因米而異。舊米吸水多而新米吸水少。故米與水之比例由 1 對 1 至 1 對1¼。至於煮飯用之器皿對用水量之影響反而不大。電飯煲、瓦鍋與不銹鋼煲之用水量皆大同小異，唯一要注意的是飯之用途與用水量有重大的關係。用以製炒飯的用水較少，約 1 對 1 至 1 對1⅛；用以當白飯的用水較多，約 1 對1⅕至 1 對1¼。每轉一隻新牌子時最好先試煮一次才定用水量。

Rice with Sausages
鴛鴦雙腸飯

Ingredients:

1½ cups rice
2 tsp salt
2 tbsp oil
2 cups water
~~2 pork sausages~~
2 liver sausages
1 spring onion

Seasoning-
1 tbsp light soy
1 tbsp dark soy
1 tbsp sugar
a pinch of pepper

Method:

* Wash and soak the rice for 20 minutes. Drain.
* Add the salt and oil to mix well with the rice. Pour into a casserole or saucepan with the water. Arrange the pork sausages on top of the rice and cover to bring to boil over low heat. Continue to simmer for 3 minutes then remove the lid to place in the liver sausages. Cover to cook for a further 15 to 20 minutes. Turn off the heat and leave to mature for 10 to 15 minutes.
* Mix the seasoning in a small bowl. Dice the spring onion. Remove and slice the sausages. Return on to the rice. Pour the sauce over the rice and sprinkle the diced spring onion on top. Serve hot in the casserole and loosen the rice with a pair of chopsticks before serving.

材料：

米 1½ 杯
鹽 2 茶匙
油 2 湯匙
水 2 杯
臘腸 2 條
潤腸 2 條
葱 1 棵

調味—
生抽 1 湯匙
老抽 1 湯匙
糖 1 湯匙
古月粉少許

製法：

* 米預先 1 小時洗淨，浸 20 分鐘，隔乾水份。

* 鹽及油拌入米中攪勻放在瓦鍋或不銹鋼保中。將水注入撥平米粒。臘腸洗淨放在米上。蓋密鍋蓋以文火慢慢煮沸。續煮 3 分鐘後揭開加入潤腸。重蓋鍋蓋文火煮 15 至 20 分鐘。熄去爐火焗 10 至 15 分鐘。

* 上桌前將調味料拌勻以小碗盛之。葱切粒亦以小碟盛之。揭開鍋蓋將鴛鴦腸取出切斜片放回飯面上，淋上調味料及灑葱粒原鍋上桌，以筷子拌鬆即可食用。

Chilli Flavoured Crisps

香 脆 辣 茨 片

Ingredients:

5 cups water
¼ cup salt
1 tbsp chicken powder
1 tbsp sugar
2 chillies
1 lb (½ kg) potatoes
½ wok oil for deep frying
a pinch of fine salt

Method:

* Place the water and salt in a saucepan and gently bring it to boil. Add the chicken powder and sugar to stir until dissolved then turn off the heat.
* Halve and deseed the chillies. Put into the salted water and leave aside to cool.
* Peel and slice the potatoes with a sharp knife into very thin pieces then soak in the cold salted water.
* Bring the oil to just boil over moderate heat. Drain and dry the potatoes with a towel. Slide the potatoes into the hot oil to deep fry until golden brown. Drain and blot the excess oil with kitchen paper then put the crisps on a plate. Sprinkle the fine salt on the crisps and serve, or leave them to cool and keep in a jar.

材料：

水 5 杯
鹽 ¼ 杯
鷄粉 1 湯匙
糖 1 湯匙
紅椒 2 隻
茨仔 1 磅（ ½ 公斤 ）
炸油 ½ 鑊
幼鹽灑面

製法：

* 水與鹽同放在保中煮沸，加入鷄粉及糖拌溶後停火。
* 紅椒分切兩邊去籽投入鹽水中，放置一旁攤凍待用。
* 茨仔去皮以利刀切成薄片。隨切隨浸於攤凍之鹽水中。
* 油 ½ 鑊以中火煮至僅沸時，將茨片撈出放在乾毛巾上吸乾水份，即滑入沸油中炸至金黃色。撈起隔去餘油，放置已墊紙之盤中。灑下幼鹽即可食用。亦可攤凍放於瓶內，隨時取食。

Sweet Red Bean
Paste Pancakes
豆 沙 鍋 餅

Ingredients:

Pastry-
3 oz (84 g) flour
2 eggs
1½ cups water
1 egg white for sealing

Filling-
1½ lb (672 g) sweet red bean paste

a few tbsp oil for shallow frying

Method:

Pastry-
* Sift the flour into a mixing bowl.
* Beat the eggs and mix with the water. Gradually stir into the flour to blend into a smooth batter. Filter through a fine sieve or a piece of linen cloth.
* Heat the frying pan and use a piece of muslin to grease it. Pour in ¼ cup batter and swirl round to cover the entire pan. Fry over low heat until set. Loosen the edge to remove the pancake on to a greased table.

Filling-
* Divide the sweet red bean paste into 12 equal portions of about 2 oz (56 g) each.

To complete-
* Place one portion of the filling in the centre of each pancake. Press lightly into a 2″ x 3″(5 cm x 7.5cm) rectangle. Fold in the four sides of the pancake and seal with the egg white to resemble an envelope.
* Slide into a heated wok to shallow fry with the oil until golden brown. Remove and drain on a piece of kitchen paper. Cut into 6 pieces and arrange on to a platter. Serve hot.

材料：

皮—
麵粉 3 安（84克）
蛋 2 隻
水1½杯
蛋白 1 隻封口

餡料—
豆沙1½磅（672克）

油數湯匙煎炸用

製法：

皮—
* 將麵粉篩於大盆中。
* 鷄蛋去壳打爛加水和匀慢慢倒入粉中拌匀後，用紗布隔去雜質及粉粒。
* 煎鍋燒紅，以布塗油。倒入粉漿¼杯搪平，慢火煎至凝結呈微黃時倒出。

餡料—
* 將豆沙分成12等份，每份約重 2 安（56克）。

完成—
* 將每塊皮平放在塗油之桌上。豆沙排放在中央，以手輕按成 2 吋 × 3 吋（5 公分×7.5公分）之長方形，皮之四邊摺入以蛋貼緊收口處按成信封狀。
* 轉放燒沸之淺油鑊中，半煎炸至兩面金黃色。撈起隔去餘油，每塊分切六件排放平碟上即可上桌。

Egg and Barley Sweet
薏米蛋糖水

Ingredients:

3 oz (84 g) pearl barley
1 cup boiling water
20 ginkgo nuts
2 beancurd sheets
10 cups water
8 oz (224 g) sugar
2 eggs

Method:

* Wash and soak the pearl barley in the boiling water for an hour. Leave aside for later use.
* Shell and soak the ginkgo nuts in hot water for 20 minutes then peel off the skin. Wash and tear the beancurd sheets into pieces.
* Bring the water to boil in a saucepan. Pour in the pearl barley, ginkgo nuts and beancurd sheet then cover to simmer over low heat for an hour. Remove the lid and add the sugar to simmer over low heat for 10 minutes till the sugar dissolves.
* Beat the eggs and trickle into the sweet soup to mix well. Serve hot or cold in small bowls.

材料：

薏米 3 安（84克）
白菓20粒
腐皮 2 張
水10杯
糖 8 安（224克）
蛋 2 隻

製法：

* 薏米洗淨浸在1杯沸水中1小時，候用。
* 白菓去壳，以溫水浸20分鐘去衣。腐皮洗淨撕碎。
* 水10杯放在保中煮沸。倒入薏米，白菓及腐皮中火保 1 小時。揭蓋加糖，文火再煮10分鐘至糖溶。
* 鷄蛋打爛加入糖水中攪匀，盛在碗內上桌。

2. Add the sugar to the boiling barley soup.

1. Soak the pearl barley in the boiling water for an hour.

3. Trickle in the beaten eggs to complete.

Papaya Milk

木 瓜 鮮 奶

Ingredients:

12 oz (336 g) papayas
4 cups cold milk
3 oz (84 g) sugar

Method:

* Chill the papayas in the refrigerator. Peel and cut them in halves. Remove the seeds with a spoon. Wash, dry and cut into large chunks. Leave aside for later use.
* Put the milk, papayas and sugar into a blender and whisk at medium speed for about 40 seconds until the milk and mashed papayas are thoroughly mixed.
* Pour the liquid into a few glasses. Serve immediately, or mix well with a cup of crushed ice and serve chilled.

材料：

木瓜12安（336克）
凍鮮奶 4 杯
糖 3 安（84克）

製法

* 木瓜雪凍去皮破開兩邊。以匙羹挖去籽，沖洗乾淨，切件候用。
* 將鮮奶、木瓜及糖一同放入攪拌器內，用中等速度打約40秒鐘至木瓜與鮮奶完全打爛和勻。
* 預備深杯數隻，將已拌妥之木瓜鮮奶倒在杯內，立刻飲用，亦可加入碎冰一杯和勻。

1. Cut the papaya in halves and remove the seeds.

2. Peel off the skin.

3. Place all the ingredients in the blender and blend on medium speed for 40 seconds.

4. Pour the liquid into the glasses and serve.

Red Bean Sweet with Quails' Eggs
鵪蛋紅豆沙

Red Bean Sweet with Quails' Eggs

鵪 蛋 紅 豆 沙

Ingredients:

5 oz (140 g) red beans
1 sq. in. (2.5 cm²) dried tangerine
  peel or fresh orange peel
6 to 7 cups water
6 oz (168 g) sugar
10 quails' eggs
1½ cups boiling water
2 tsp cornflour
  + 2 tbsp water (optional)

Method:

* Wash, rinse and drain the red beans. Wash and soak the tangerine peel in ¼ cup of hot water.
* Fill a 3-quart saucepan with the water. Pour in the red beans and the peel to bring to the boil. Simmer over medium heat for 1 hour until softened.
* Place the red beans into a blender or food processor and blend it into a smooth purée. Return to the saucepan and add the sugar to reboil till dissolved.
* Boil the quails' eggs in a small saucepan with the boiling water for 3 minutes. Remove and put under a running tap to rinse till cold. Shell.
* Mix the cornflour with the water then trickle into the sweet soup to thicken the consistency.
* Place the shelled eggs into the sweet soup while it is still boiling. Turn off the heat and scoop into a soup tureen.

材料：

紅豆 5 安（140克）
陳皮或橙皮 1 方吋
水 6 至 7 杯
冰糖或沙糖 6 安（168克）
鵪蛋10隻
沸水 1½ 杯
生粉 2 茶匙＋水 2 湯匙（隨意）

製法：

* 將紅豆清洗乾淨隔去水份。陳皮洗淨用熱水浸軟。
* 將紅豆、水及陳皮一同放在不銹鋼煲或瓦鍋內煮沸後轉用中火續煮 1 小時至鬆軟。
* 紅豆取出放在碎肉機或攪拌器內攪成茸。將豆沙重放煲中加糖煮至糖溶。
* 鵪蛋放在鍋中煮 3 分鐘，取出冲凍後去壳。
* 生粉加水和勻慢慢流入紅豆沙內，拌至濃度適中再滾時，將鵪蛋放入。熄去爐火倒在湯窩內上桌。

These are the ingredients
for the dish:—
1 sugar
2 water
3 red beans
4 soaked tangerine peel
5 quails' eggs
6 dried tangerine peel

1. Grind the cooked red beans in a food processor.

2. Poach the quails' eggs in the boiling water for 3 minutes.

3. Allow the eggs to cool and shell.

4. Return the bean puree into the saucepan.

5. Add the sugar to simmer till dissolved.

6. Slide in the eggs and serve.

Sugar Cane and Water Chestnut Beverage
馬蹄竹蔗水

Ingredients:

½ lb (224 g) water chestnuts
1 lb (½ kg) sugar cane
½ lb (224 g) carrots
1 parsley sprig
8 cups water

Method:

* Wash and peel the water chest-nuts. Refresh and drain.
* Section the sugar cane into 12″ (30 cm) lengths. Peel, rinse and slice into thin strips. Scrub and slice the carrots. Wash and trim the parsley.
* Pour the water into a deep saucepan or casserole and place over medium heat to bring to boil. Add the water chestnuts, sugar cane and carrots and lower the heat to simmer for an hour. Remove the lid, put in the parsley and turn off the heat when the water reboils. Leave the drink aside to cool, then pour into the bottles to store. Chill in the refrigerator and serve cold.

N.B. You can ask the sugar cane vendor to chop and peel the sugar cane for you.

材料：

馬蹄½磅（224克）
竹蔗1磅（½公斤）
甘筍½磅（224克）
芫茜1棵
水8杯

製法：

* 馬蹄洗淨削去皮再沖乾淨，以笒箕盛着隔去水份。
* 竹蔗斬成12吋（30公分）段削去皮沖洗後刨成薄片。甘筍去皮切片。芫茜洗淨摘妥。
* 深鍋或瓦保一個。將水注入，放在中火爐上煮沸。加入馬蹄、竹蔗、甘筍，轉用文火續煮1小時。揭蓋放下芫茜，待重沸時即可離火，攤凍後盛在瓶中置雪柜內作凍飲。

註：竹蔗可要求賣蔗者代斬及去皮、切段。

Chinese Cookery Terms

1. **To BAKE** is to cook with dry heat, or to dry food with heat.
2. **To BARBEQUE** is to cook meat over a charcoal or wood fire.
3. **To BIND** is to add egg, liquid or melted fat to a mixture in order to hold it together.
4. **To BLANCH** is to immerse the food in boiling water for a short time (from 10 seconds to 5 minutes) in order to tighten the texture, set the colour, or get rid of any unpleasant smell of the food.
5. **To BOIL** is to cook the food in hot bubbling liquid.
6. **To BRAISE** is to finish cooking in a tightly covered wok or saucepan.
7. **To CRIMP** is to slash the surface of a fish at intervals.
8. **To DEEP FRY** is to cook food in a large amount of hot boiling oil in order to make it crispy.
9. **To DOUBLE-BOIL** is to cook in a covered container, which is placed in a covered wok half-filled with boiling water.
10. **To DRAIN** is to remove excess liquid from the ingredients through a strainer or colander.
11. **To DREDGE** is to sprinkle the ingredient with flour or sugar, etc.
12. **To FRY** is to cook with a little hot oil.
13. **To GUT** is to remove the intestine and clean the inside of a fish.
14. **To PARBOIL** is to leave the food in warm oil until half-cooked.
15. **To PARCH** is to brown food in a dry hot wok or frying pan.
16. **To POACH** is to simmer food gently in a liquid which is kept just below boiling point.
17. **To REFRESH** is to rinse the ingredient with cold water after it is blanched. The ingredient is then reheated before serving.
18. **To ROAST** is to prepare the food by using high heat, with flame or over the charcoal.
19. **To SAUTÉ** is to stir the ingredients quickly in a wok or pan with a little hot oil, over high heat.
20. **To SCALD** is to plunge the ingredient into boiling water quickly to make peeling easier or to clean or loosen the hair on the ingredient.
21. **To SHALLOW FRY** is to cook the food in a little oil until both sides are brown.
22. **To SIMMER** is to cook the food or liquid slowly over low heat.
23. **To SMOKE** is to place the food on a rack in a wok or oven filled with smoke.
24. **To STEAM** is to cook the food by putting it into a steamer placed in a wok half-filled with boiling water. Timing begins when the water boils. High heat should be used so that there is enough steam to cook the food quickly.
25. **To STEW** is to cook the food with a little liquid over low heat.
26. **To STIR FRY** is to cook the food quickly in a little oil over medium heat.
27. **To TOSS** is to mix the ingredients evenly by throwing them in a wok and jerking the wok up and down.

The cooking oil used in this book can either be corn oil, vegetable oil, peanut oil or sunflower oil, unless otherwise stated.

烹飪常用術語

焗　　—將食物放鑊中蓋密，以文火焗熟。或將拌妥粉料放焗爐中以慢火焗至鬆發。

炭燒　—將食物以叉叉着或放在炭上之鐵網直接以明火燒熟。

搞　　—加水或蛋或牛奶在乾材料中和成一糰。

飛水　—將食物放入沸水內稍拖一下，取出洗淨續煮。

焓　　—將食物放入沸水中，藉沸水熱力使食品煮熟。與灼及煮略同。灼要手快。

紅燒　—用豉油及水將食物煮熟。與煮及炆略同，有時則與烤之意義相近如燒烤。

炸　　—將大量油煮沸，放入食物浸過面，以沸油之熱度使食物炸至酥脆。油炸食品多需上
　　　　乾粉或濕粉，並要猛油落鑊。

燉　　—將食物加配料及水放在燉盅內，再轉放深鍋中加水慢火燉至食品酥爛。食前加調味
　　　　。此法可保原味，多與補品同燉。

上粉　—將食物以麵粉或糖酒勻在週圍而後按實。

炒　　—將鑊燒紅，加少量油煮沸，放入材料迅速兜勻。

泡油　—將食物醃好後，放入猛鑊陰油中泡至油將沸時撈起，隔去油候用。

烙　　—以燒熱乾鑊將已洗淨材料文火煮乾後續烙至淺黃色。

浸　　—用湯或油煮沸後將火降至將沸未沸之溫度，把食物如鷄或魚等放入，以一定之溫度
　　　　浸至熟，切不可用猛火。

過冷河—將食物先用沸水煮過，取出再放冷水中沖凍使其爽脆，麵食多須過冷河。

烤　　—以明火將食物炙熟使香氣四溢，用中式烤爐與西式焗爐皆可。

爆　　—迅速用猛火將食物以油或醬料加料頭用火逼熟。

灼或燙—將食物迅速放入沸水中浸片刻然後去皮或拔毛。

煎　　—燒紅鑊放少量油將食物僅浸到少許，慢火煎至兩面金黃香脆。

燴　　—燒熱油鑊，讚酒加上湯，再加已泡油或煮熟之食物及配料煮沸，以粟粉開水少許打
　　　　饂。

焗或燻—食物先用調味品醃過，排在已放燻料（糖、蔗片、茶葉等）之鑊中的鐵絲網上。
　　　　蓋上鑊蓋，藉燻料冒出之烟使食物燻至微黃而有烟味。

蒸　　—將食物以碟盛起放蒸籠內蓋密，轉置沸水鑊中以蒸氣使食物致熟。

炆　　—先將食物放配料爆炒過，轉放另一密蓋鑊內加水少許，改用文火經長時間炆至食物
　　　　酥爛汁濃為止。紅炆者熟後加老抽。

拌炒　—此為中國烹飪中最常用之方法，將食物先泡嫩油至七分熟，然後再燒紅鑊加配料放
　　　　食物讚酒，迅速兜勻上碟。

拋　　—將鑊中食物迅速在大火上拋動，使火力平均。

煮　　—將食物放入水中煮，藉沸水之熱力將食品煮至酥爛，然後加調味料。

保　　—將食物放入水中煮滾，改用文火繼續保至夠火及出味為止。此法通常需時較長。

滷　　—用水加滷水料、生抽、紹酒、冰糖等煮至出味。然後把食物飛水後浸在滷水中。浸
　　　　至入味。滷水盆如處理得宜可長期不變壞。

煨　　—將食物放入上湯內慢火煮之，使其吸收上湯味道，或放羗葱水內煨之，以除腥味。

撈拌　—把已煮熟之食物切絲與其他配料放在一起和勻謂之撈。多用於冷盆。

扒　　—手法與燴略同，唯汁水較少及較濃。

註：本書食譜內所用之油通常為粟米油，亦可用菜油或花生油。

CHOPSTICKS PUBLICATIONS LTD.

CHOPSTICKS PUBLICATIONS LTD. has been established for many years and specialises in high quality cookery books and cookery cards on Chinese cuisine. The author of the **CHOPSTICKS RECIPES** series — Mrs. Cecilia J. Au-yeung — continues to research and develop new recipes for the compilation of more cookery books.

Mrs. Cecilia J. Au-yeung graduated in Domestic Science from the Hong Kong Grantham Teachers' Training College in 1956 and was immediately appointed by the Hong Kong Education Department to teach at the Hong Kong and Kowloon Restaurant and Teahouse Employee's Guild School. Since then the author has gained valuable knowledge of cooking from many famous Chinese chefs. In 1971 Mrs. Au-yeung embarked on a career editing recipes for several established local magazines and newspapers. In the same year she also started the Chopsticks Cooking Centre to provide the best facilities for learning Chinese cooking. It was in 1975 that the publishing company was established to publish Mrs. Au-yeung's recipes in English and Chinese. Her husband Mr. Wilson Au-yeung developed a keen interest in photography in his youth and eventually turned professional in 1960. He then undertook to take all the photographs for the cookery books. In 1984, Mrs. Au-yeung combined her extensive experience as a cookery writer with her husband's skills as a photographer to produce a cookery book for Hamlyn Publishing.

In 1985, Mrs. Au-yeung began to write her new series of cookery books for parents and children to learn Chinese cooking together. The first two books of this series are **FIRST STEPS IN CHINESE COOKING** and **MORE STEPS IN CHINESE COOKING.**

Besides publishing cookery books, Chopsticks Publications Ltd. has also started to publish books on travel in China.

嘉饌出版有限公司簡介

嘉饌出版有限公司於一九七五年十二月成立至今已有十年歷史，爲本港唯一專門出版優質中英對照食譜書集之出版社。作者歐陽紉詩女士乃葛量洪師範學院家政系畢業生。於一九七一年在課餘時間創辦嘉饌家政中心教授中西烹飪及餅食。積十餘年之豐富經驗從而將食譜編集成書。其外子歐陽榮先生乃一資深之業餘攝影師，以三十多年心得，拍攝書集內令人垂涎欲滴，呼之欲出之圖片。

嘉饌之烹飪叢書「美點佳餚」迄今已出版十一册。第十二册將於八六年年底出版。此外，嘉饌亦曾出版兩册「美食初階」烹飪咭，特別爲中學之家政學生及初學烹飪者而設。八四年十二月出版之「美鑊飄香」則是一部全新製作，特別介紹用中國鑊作烹飪之各種用途。本年度該公司將於十二月推出兩册「美食入門」食譜，專爲兒童精心編著，使能共享與父母一同下廚之樂趣。

嘉饌出版之烹飪書彩圖鮮艷，內容充實，印刷精美，價錢超值。暢銷本港及世界各地。選購聖誕，新年或生辰禮物，何必多傷腦筋？「美點佳餚」將使你的親友永遠感謝您！記着您！

同時，嘉饌特別爲讀者設立了一個解決疑難的部門。舉凡有採購材料及用具或技術上之難題，皆可由該部門或嘉饌家政中心之導師負責解答。